iPhone® 5 Kickstart

Dennis Cohen
Michael Cohen

New York   Chicago   San Francisco
Lisbon   London   Madrid   Mexico City
Milan   New Delhi   San Juan
Seoul   Singapore   Sydney   Toronto

The **McGraw·Hill** Companies

Cataloging-in-Publication Data is on file with the Library of Congress

McGraw-Hill books are available at special quantity discounts to use as premiums and sales promotions, or for use in corporate training programs. To contact a representative, please e-mail us at bulksales@mcgraw-hill.com.

iPhone® 5 Kickstart

1 2 3 4 5 6 7 8 9 0   DOC DOC   1 0 9 8 7 6 5 4 3 2

ISBN   978-0-07-180985-6
MHID   0-07-180985-6

SPONSORING EDITOR	**TECHNICAL EDITOR**	**PRODUCTION SUPERVISOR**
Megg Morin	Jill Duffy	Jean Bodeaux
EDITORIAL SUPERVISOR	**COPY EDITOR**	**COMPOSITION**
Jody McKenzie	Lisa Theobald	Cenveo Publisher Services
PROJECT MANAGER	**PROOFREADER**	**ILLUSTRATION**
Sheena Uprety,	Julie Searls	Cenveo Publisher Services
Cenveo Publisher Services	**INDEXER**	**ART DIRECTOR, COVER**
ACQUISITIONS COORDINATOR	Jack Lewis	Jeff Weeks
Stephanie Evans		

Dennis would like to dedicate his efforts here to his wonderful wife, Kathy, who dragged him (kicking and screaming) into cell phone usage a year before the iPhone's introduction, and to Apple for the iPhone, the first cell phone he didn't hate and the one that has become his constant companion.

ACKNOWLEDGMENTS

Dennis would like to acknowledge Michael, whose vision and humor make writing a book like this on a tight schedule bearable and, at times, enjoyable. Thanks also to the folks at McGraw-Hill who shepherded us through the effort: Megg, Stephanie, and Jill. Finally, thanks to our agent, Carole Jelen, for making the introduction.

Michael would like to acknowledge Dennis (of course), our editors, and our agent, and to offer special thanks to Adam and Tonya Engst and the rest of the TidBITS staff and the Control Freaks who made it possible for him to devote the time he needed to work on this book.

About the Authors

Dennis Cohen has 35 years in the "software biz" as a developer, development manager, consultant, technical editor (more than 400 titles), and author (more than 30 titles), starting out in the Jet Propulsion Laboratory's Deep Space Network in the late 1970s, with stints at Ashton-Tate, Apple/Claris, and Aladdin Systems along the way.

Michael Cohen has been living at the intersection of technology and the humanities for his entire professional life. Over the years, he has taught English composition, worked as a programmer for NASA's Deep Space Network, helped to develop the first commercial ebooks at the Voyager Company (no relation to NASA's *Voyager*, by the way), co-founded a major university's Humanities computing center, written a number of books and articles, and played with a lot of new technology while pretending it was "for work" (yeah, right).

About the Technical Editor

Jill Duffy is a writer and software analyst at *PC Magazine*. She also writes a weekly column about staying organized in a digital world at www.pcmag.com/get-organized.

CONTENTS

PART III

Sync and Share Data

PART IV

Obtain Digital Media

PART V

Use the Cameras

INTRODUCTION

This book, *iPhone 5 Kickstart,* is a consolidated guide to the latest incarnation of Apple's industry-defining smartphone. It is designed to give you what you need to know to use your new iPhone easily and enjoyably, briefing you on its myriad features and capabilities without slowing you down with technical discussions.

In Part I of this book, we help you get started with your iPhone:

- Chapter 1 shows you how to set up your new device, helps you make some essential settings, and gives you a tour of what's in the box.

- Chapter 2 explains how to place calls on the iPhone and make use of its flexible onscreen keyboard for typing and editing. In this chapter you also get to meet Siri, the iPhone's intelligent assistant who can answer a variety of questions and perform many tasks for you.

- Chapter 3 shows you how you can get e-mail from one or more e-mail accounts, how to send e-mail, and how to organize your mail.

- Chapter 4 takes you to the Web with the iPhone's powerful mobile Safari browser and shows you how to make use of its tabbed browsing, shared bookmarks, and reading list capabilities.

- Chapter 5 shepherds you on a whirlwind tour of the many apps that come bundled with your iPhone, ranging from old favorites such as the Weather app and Calculator to the newest apps such as Passbook, which allows you to store boarding passes, movie tickets, and store coupons in one place.

In Part II, we cover the iPhone's communication features and capabilities in more detail:

- Chapter 6 looks at more advanced phone features such as favorites and ringtones, explains how to use call waiting and call forwarding, describes the iPhone's unique Visual Voicemail feature, and shows you how to make conference calls.

- Chapter 7 covers the apps that help you stay in touch and on time: your Contacts and Calendar apps. We show you how to use your contacts with the Mail app, make phone calls, and find them on a map, and we cover how to use your Calendar to create appointments, set alerts, and assign your Calendar events to specialized calendars.

- Chapter 8 covers even more communication avenues, including text and media messaging, video chats using Apple's FaceTime technology, and touching base with family, friends, and co-workers via Twitter and Facebook.

Part III is devoted to helping you get your information in order:

- Chapter 9 explains how to use iTunes to get your music, photos, books, bookmarks, contacts, calendars, and more synchronized between your computer and your iPhone.

- Chapter 10 takes to the air to explain how you can use iCloud and other online services to keep your information synchronized as well—without wires.

Part IV is all about media and apps:

- In Chapter 11 we take you on a shopping trip to the App Store and show you how to browse for apps, search for specific ones, download them, and restore them if you happen to delete them.

- Chapter 12 takes you to the iTunes Store and shows you how to find music, movies, videos, TV shows, and more. In this chapter you also learn how to use the Music app for playing and organizing your audio purchases and the Videos app for playing movies and TV shows.

- Chapter 13 invites you to sit back and read a good book or magazine and explains how to use the iBooks app for reading books, the iBookstore for purchasing them, and the Newsstand app for organizing your collection of digital periodicals, along with some pointers to other useful and enjoyable reading apps.

Part V covers the advanced camera capabilities of your iPhone:

- Chapter 14 describes how to use the cameras (yes, the iPhone has two of them) to take stunning still photos and panoramas. It also covers how to manage and share your photo collection with the Photos app.

- Chapter 15 does for video what the Chapter 14 does for still photos, explaining how to plan, shoot, and edit high-quality digital video with your iPhone.

Finally, in our troubleshooting Appendix, we cover some useful techniques for those times when things don't always work right, including how to restart your iPhone as well as create a backup, and how to use the multitasking bar to tame unresponsive or misbehaving apps.

Conventions Used in this Book

Now You Know The Now You Know sidebars provide deeper detail on a topic or specifics for accomplishing a task.

Tip Tips help you make the most of your iPhone 5 by offering shortcuts or ways to streamline and super-charge your iPhone 5 experience.

Note Notes aim to draw your attention to supplemental information, background steps, or additional requirements.

Caution Keep a sharp eye out for the Caution icon to help you steer clear of potential pitfalls or problems that may lie ahead.

Part I

Get Started with Your New iPhone

1

Set Up Your New iPhone

Congratulations on getting your new iPhone. In this chapter, we'll describe what you should have found in the box (in addition to your new iPhone), explain how to activate the iPhone with your mobile service carrier so that you can make phone calls, and help you enable the essential settings so that you can get down to work—or play—with your new iPhone as quickly as possible. We'll also cover what role Apple's iTunes application has in helping you manage your iPhone's contents (including whether or not you need to use iTunes at all), and we'll give you a quick briefing on iOS, the software that turns

Now You Know — What Is iOS?

Throughout this book, you'll see the letters *iOS* from time to time. iOS is the name of the *operating system*, the software that controls the workings and that provides the basic features of your iPhone. The apps that you purchase as well as those that come with the iPhone require many of the services provided by iOS in order to work. The onscreen keyboard, for example, is provided by iOS, as is the Home screen you see, the passcode lock you use, and much more. From time to time, Apple issues updates to iOS, which you can download and install on your iPhone. We talk about how to install iOS updates in the Appendix.

the iPhone from an inert but attractive assemblage of metal, glass, and silicon into one of the most popular and versatile mobile smartphones on the planet.

Unpack Your iPhone

Inside the small box that contains your iPhone are a couple of accessories that no iPhone user should be without, as shown in Figure 1-1.

The Apple EarPods may look similar to the earbuds that accompany other devices, but they do more than simply deliver sound to your ears. You can click the small remote control on the right cable to control audio volume, to advance from track to track when you use your iPhone as a music player, and to put calls on hold or switch between calls when you use your iPhone as a phone. In addition, the remote control includes a tiny microphone so you can talk on your phone even while it is in your pocket.

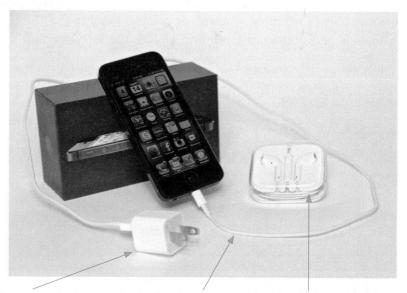

USB power adapter   Lightning connector cable   Apple EarPods with inline
                                                        microphone and control

Figure 1-1   *What's in the box*

The other two pieces of hardware that come with your iPhone are designed to work together: a Universal Serial Bus (USB) power adapter that can plug into standard 120-volt electrical outlets, and a Lightning connector-to-USB cable. Plug the USB end of the cable into the power adapter and the Lightning connector end into the socket at the bottom of your iPhone, and your iPhone immediately begins charging. Unlike the Dock connecter used on previous iPhones, iPads, and iPods since 2003 that fit into the socket only one way, the new Lightning connector fits either way and is much narrower. Apple has announced that this connector will be used for the foreseeable future on all of its portable devices.

You also use the Lightning connector to connect your iPhone to your computer so you can both charge the iPhone using your computer's power and sync information between your computer and your iPhone. (We cover syncing in Part 3.) If you prefer to set up your iPhone by connecting it to iTunes instead of wirelessly (we describe both methods a little later in this chapter), you'll use the Lightning connector cable to connect your iPhone to your computer as well.

In most cases, a completely uncharged iPhone can charge to full capacity in just a few hours. However, you may not need to charge your iPhone when you first receive it. As shipped by Apple, the iPhone starts out completely charged, and even if it has been sitting on a shelf in an Apple Store or mobile carrier store for awhile, or traveling by plane and truck from Apple to you, chances are that it still retains more than enough charge for you to activate it and begin using it. Nonetheless, if you can manage your impatience, you should take the time to charge your iPhone fully before you activate it, just to be on the safe side: you don't want your iPhone to go dark with a depleted battery just as you are about to use it for the first time!

And while you are waiting to top off the iPhone's capacious lithium-ion internal battery, you can amuse yourself by reading the documentation that comes with your iPhone. There's not much there, so you'll have time to read it twice or more.

Activate and Set Up Your iPhone

Before you can use your iPhone, you must *activate* it. Activation involves connecting your iPhone with your mobile service provider so you can make phone calls and use the provider's data network. Even if you're not changing carriers, you still need to transfer your phone number from your old device to your new iPhone. Activation also includes establishing an Apple ID (or logging in with an existing Apple ID) so that Apple and your phone can communicate with each other—essential if you want to purchase apps, music, books, or video.

Furthermore, during these steps you can choose to establish an iCloud account with Apple if you want (and you really should, because it's free and a lot of useful features aren't available without it): iCloud comprises several services from Apple with which you can sync information across your iPhone and other Apple devices, using Apple's remote servers. iCloud helps ensure that you can retrieve important information any time you have an Internet connection, including backups of your iPhone's data, music, and documents that you create, as well as calendars, contacts, e-mail, and other useful stuff.

Although the activation process involves several steps, they are not difficult, and Apple provides clear on-screen instructions for every step. Nonetheless, we describe each step in the following pages and provide some extra explanation of what those steps mean and what they do.

 If you purchased your iPhone at a retail Apple Store or your mobile provider's store, the staff there can help you activate your iPhone.

Initial Activation Steps

At the very top of your iPhone, on the right as you face it, is an oblong button, known by various names: Power, On/Off, and Sleep/Wake being the most common. We're going to call it the Sleep/Wake button, because that's what it does when you press it, unless you hold it down for a few seconds. If your iPhone is powered off, you actually do have to hold it down for a couple seconds until you see the Apple logo appear, followed by the screen shown in Figure 1-2.

Place your finger on the slider labeled "Slide To Set Up" (it's in Kanji in the figure) and slide it to the right. You will be greeted by a bit of Apple fluff, a screen with the word "Welcome" in multiple languages, as shown in Figure 1-3, and a list of languages from which to choose for menus, prompts, and so on. If the language you want isn't present on this first screen, tap the down-pointing arrow and a longer list of languages appears. To look for entries further down the list, place your finger on the list and slide (or *flick*) upward to reveal other choices. This sliding or flicking is a gesture that you will find useful on your iPhone; it's how you scroll through lists, menus, and screens that are too long to fit on your iPhone's display.

Figure 1-2   *iPhone screen, ready for setup*

Figure 1-3   *Select the language you want your iPhone to use.*

Tap a language to choose it. Then tap Next. The Country or Region screen appears (see Figure 1-4). Proceed as you did when specifying the language—tap your location. Your iPhone uses this information to select the dictionary it uses when you dictate and when it auto-completes or auto-corrects your typing. Once you've chosen a country or region, tap Next to see the Location Services screen also shown in Figure 1-4.

This screen offers you the choices of enabling or disabling Location Services, which provides the information used to record the location of photos you take, to set the time zone to use for your time display, to help give you directions with the Map app, and to provide information to any other app or feature for which your location is germane. Tap your choice (we recommend you enable Location Services; you can

Figure 1-4 *Choose your country or region and then enable Location Services to let iPhone apps use your location.*

always turn it off later), and then tap Next to proceed to the Wi-Fi networks screen (Figure 1-5).

Setup: Via Computer or Wireless?

Now it's time to make a decision that affects the rest of the setup process: Do you set up your iPhone using iTunes on a Mac or Windows computer, or do you set it up wirelessly, untethered from a personal computer? If possible, especially if you have content such as songs, videos, and photos on your computer, we recommend setting up through iTunes on your computer (and this is generally faster). Additionally, if you have a lot of audio and video that you didn't purchase through the iTunes Store, you'll find that using iTunes is less

Figure 1-5   *The Wi-Fi screen lets you choose a network with which to connect to the Internet.*

expensive than paying for storage beyond the 5GB that is free with an iCloud account.

If you choose the wireless route, and your Wi-Fi network is listed on the Wi-Fi screen (Figure 1-5), read the "Set Up Using Wireless or Wi-Fi on Your iPhone" section; otherwise, skip ahead to the section, "Set Up Using iTunes on Your Computer."

Set Up Using Wireless or Wi-Fi on Your iPhone
On the Wi-Fi Networks screen, tap the name of your network to connect to it. If the network name shows a padlock icon, it means you have to enter a password to make the connection.

When a chosen Wi-Fi network requires a password, the iPhone's on-screen keyboard appears so you can enter it. Tap the password, tapping the Shift (up-arrow) key when a capital letter is required and tapping the numeric keyboard key (lower-left corner) when you need to enter a number or punctuation symbol (such as an underscore, period, or minus/plus sign). To return to the alphabetic keyboard, tap the ABC key. (We tell you more—much more—about how to use the iPhone's various keyboards in Chapter 2.)

Next, you need to choose between setting up your iPhone as a new iPhone or restoring it from a saved backup.

- If you're a new iPhone user, skip ahead to the section, "Create a New Apple ID or Use an Existing Apple ID."

- If you're restoring from a backup, you already know what iTunes and/or iCloud is and how to use them, so make your choice, follow the prompts, and then skip the rest of this setup material.

Set Up Using iTunes on Your Computer

If you have a Mac, you have iTunes, so you're good to go, barring a possible need to update to the latest version. When you launch iTunes on your Mac, it will check in with Apple's servers and inform you whether an update is available; proceed with the update.

When you use a Windows PC, you don't necessarily have iTunes installed. You will have it if you have an iPod, Apple TV, or any of a myriad of other Apple products, or if you chose to use it as your media center. (In our opinion, iTunes is far superior to the music player that comes with Windows, and, because iTunes is free, there is no reason not to install it.) If you don't already have iTunes, go to www.apple.com/iTunes and follow the prompts to download and install it.

Once you have iTunes running, insert the Lightning connector end of the cable into the port at the bottom of your iPhone and plug the USB end of the cable into a USB port on your computer or a powered hub.

The iPhone will shortly appear under the DEVICES category in the iTunes source list (the sidebar at the left side of the iTunes window).

Select the iPhone's entry and the Set Up iPhone screen appears in the iTunes main pane. You can name your iPhone here, as well as choose whether iTunes should automatically synchronize your data in related applications, such as your contacts (Contacts or Address Book on the Mac, Outlook in Windows), e-mail accounts, calendars, and web browser bookmarks, as well as any apps that you might already have in iTunes' database. Make your choices and click Done. iTunes proceeds with the setup process, contacting your cellular provider and authorizing the device (this can take a few minutes).

Set Up Using iCloud

In the Set Up iPhone screen (Figure 1-6), tap Set Up As New iPhone, and then tap Next. Your iPhone contacts your mobile service provider and goes through the authorization process as depicted in Figure 1-7, where you're informed that it can take a few minutes.

Figure 1-6   *Tap Set Up As New iPhone.*

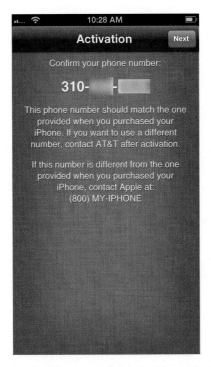

Figure 1-7   *Sit back and wait while your cellular provider authorizes your iPhone.*

Create a New Apple ID or Use an Existing Apple ID

When authorization is complete, the Apple ID screen shown in Figure 1-8 appears. We know what you're now thinking: What *is* an Apple ID?

Apple IDs consist of a user name (in the form of an e-mail address) and a password (*not* your e-mail password, but a different one that you create and that is used to verify the Apple ID whenever you need to use it). If you've ever purchased anything through one of Apple's online stores or have another Apple device, you almost certainly have an Apple ID. If that is the case, tap Sign In With An Apple ID and supply your Apple ID and password using the on-screen keyboard that appears.

Figure 1-8 *Use an existing Apple ID or create a new one.*

 If you're curious about what an Apple ID is or how and for what it can be used, tap the What Is An Apple ID link at the bottom of the Apple ID screen.

If you don't already have an Apple ID (or if you want to create a new one), tap Create A Free Apple ID and follow the prompts. At the end of the Apple ID creation process, you are asked to agree to Apple's Terms and Conditions. Read those terms and conditions if you like, but, whether you do or not, go ahead and agree: you won't be able to use most of your iPhone's most interesting and fun features if you don't have an Apple ID.

Sign Up for iCloud

After you specify your Apple ID, your iPhone asks you about signing up for iCloud. And, again, we know what you're thinking: What is iCloud?

iCloud is a free, online set of services and applications that can make your digital life easier. As it says on the Set Up iCloud screen, iCloud can store your photos, apps, contacts, calendars, and more, and it can send them wirelessly to your iPhone. Apple gives you 5GB of storage to house this data for free, and if you need more space, you can buy it. That 5GB is in addition to any apps or media purchased through Apple's various iTunes Store departments, the photos in your PhotoStream (which we cover in detail in Chapter 14), or any media under the aegis of the optional iTunes Match service (covered in Chapter 12). It also provides you with an e-mail address—it never hurts to have another e-mail address or three. We recommend you tap the Use iCloud button and then tap Next and follow the prompts that appear.

Choose a Backup Strategy

Assuming that you followed the prompts and have created an iCloud account, you now decide whether you want your iPhone to back up daily when charging your iPhone within range of a Wi-Fi network, or to back up to iTunes, which can be done via the USB connection to your computer or wirelessly to your computer—if your computer is turned on, awake, and iTunes is running on it.

The major advantages for backing up to iTunes are that it is faster and it does not limit the amount of data you can back up—remember that iCloud gives you only 5GB space total for all your data, which includes backups. Another iTunes advantage is that if you use OS X's Time Machine backup facility or various Windows backup utilities, your backup has a backup.

 We know that losing data is traumatic, and personal data such as photos are often irreplaceable. Backups are crucial, because there are two types of computer users: those who have lost data and those who will lose data, probably at the most inconvenient possible time.

The big advantage of backing up to iCloud is that it is available anywhere you have an Internet connection. And don't be afraid of that 5GB limit: for many users, the 5GB (which you can increase for a fee, as described in Chapter 10) can be more than enough storage space for all your data. For one thing, it applies only to data that *you* create or acquire from a source other than one of Apple's stores. Content purchased through the iTunes Store (discussed in Part 4) doesn't count against that 5GB. Only your own videos, documents, calendars, and so forth are included as part of the 5GB. Nonetheless, if, for example, you plan to shoot videos with your iPhone camera (and you well might—it is a fine camera), keep in mind that those videos can take up a lot of storage space: for videographers, an iTunes backup is a cheaper—and faster—way to protect your data.

Final Setup Steps

Once you have chosen how you want to back up your iPhone, you are asked if you want to use the Find My iPhone function. This function, which is another service provided by iCloud, works with Location Services to help you track down a misplaced (or stolen) iPhone, send a message to whoever has found your iPhone, and, if necessary, remotely erase all the iPhone's content to protect you from having your personal information wind up in the hands of strangers. The Find My iPhone feature of iCloud is also available to iPads, iPod touches, and Mac computers (appropriately renamed).

Finally, you're asked whether your iPhone should send diagnostic data to Apple on a daily basis. This data can include information such as your iPhone's location and, if a Wi-Fi connection is not available, transmitting the data could take a bite out of your mobile data allocation. Whether you want to help Apple improve its product at the cost of revealing where you are and your possibly paying for the privilege is up to you.

Enable Essential Settings

At this point, your iPhone is ready for you to enjoy. However, we recommend that you immediately use the Settings app to make sure that a couple of settings are configured for your protection.

To use the Settings app, on the *Home screen* that appears (as shown next) when the setup process concludes, tap the Settings icon. (We tell you more about the iPhone's Home screens and how to manage them in Chapter 5.)

The Settings app gives you access to iPhone settings and the various apps included on your iPhone. A lot of settings are available, but here we'll discuss only a couple of them. The main screen of the Settings app is shown in Figure 1-9.

First, you want to make sure that you can control how loud your iPhone rings with the volume buttons on the left side of the iPhone. Here's how to do that:

1. Tap Sounds to reveal the Sounds settings (Figure 1-10).

2. Make sure the Change With Buttons switch is On (it should be).

3. At the top of the Sounds settings screen, tap Settings. This returns you to the main Settings screen.

Figure 1-9 *The main screen of the Settings app*

The next setting you want to configure is how long your iPhone can sit idly until it goes to sleep. Here's what to do:

1. On the main Settings screen, tap General to open the General settings screen.

2. Swipe down until you can see the Auto-Lock setting, and then tap it.

3. Tap one of the time settings (to save battery life, we usually choose a short time, such as one or two minutes), and then, at the top of the screen, tap General.

Finally, to make it just a little more difficult for someone else to use your iPhone without your permission, you should set a Passcode Lock. A Passcode Lock requires that you enter either a four-digit number or a

Figure 1-10   *The Sounds settings screen*

variable-length phrase (if you turn off Simple Passcode) to unlock the
iPhone when you wake it up. Here, we show you how to set up a simple
Passcode Lock:

1. On the General screen, swipe down until you see Passcode Lock,
   and then tap it.

2. On the Passcode Lock screen, make sure that Simple Passcode is
   switched On; if it isn't, tap the onscreen On/Off switch.

3. At the top of the Passcode Lock screen, tap Turn Passcode On,
   and then using the on-screen keypad that appears, tap a four-
   digit number. (Make sure it is a number you will remember!)

4. Enter the passcode again when you are asked to confirm it. The
   Passcode Lock screen reappears.

5. Tap the Require Passcode item, and choose how long your phone can remain asleep before it requires a passcode to wake it up. (We usually choose 5 minutes, since it is a pain to re-enter the passcode every time we accidentally let the phone fall asleep briefly—but let your own circumstances and preferences guide you here.)

6. At the top of the Require Passcode screen, tap Passcode Lock, and then, on the Passcode Lock screen, tap General. Finally, at the top of the General screen, tap Settings. This returns you to the main Settings screen.

7. Press the Home button—the big round button below your iPhone's screen—to return to the Home screen.

Now take a brief break before we show you how to type and talk using your iPhone, coming right up in the next chapter.

2

Talk and Type

As you know, and as we'll show you throughout this book, there's a lot you can do with your iPhone. You can do so much, in fact, that it's easy to forget that the iPhone is a mobile phone! But it is a phone—and a good one, too, with all the features you want in a mobile phone, including voicemail, call waiting, redial, and more. It's easy to dial and to send text messages with your iPhone, even though it doesn't have a physical keypad or keyboard—but it does have virtual versions of both that appear when you need them.

This chapter shows you how to use your iPhone as a phone, how to use its virtual touch-sensitive keypad and keyboard, and how to skip using the keypad and keyboard and just tell your iPhone what you want to do.

Make a Phone Call

Once you have activated your iPhone with your mobile service provider, as explained in Chapter 1, it's ready for you to make phone calls: just dial a number, hold the phone up to your ear, and start talking. Simple enough when described generally, and simple enough in practice, too. However, here are some useful details that can help you make the most of your first call.

How to Hold the iPhone When Making Calls

First, you need to know where you talk and where you listen. Make sure that the Sleep/Wake button is at the top of the iPhone as you hold it to your ear and that you hold the phone so that the top of screen is against your ear: that way, the small speaker (the *receiver*) is positioned properly for you to hear the person you are calling. (See Figure 2-1.)

 Near the top of the iPhone screen is a small sensor that detects when your iPhone is held against your ear. This sensor turns the screen lighting off when the iPhone is against your ear so you don't waste battery power. As soon as you move the iPhone away from your ear, the screen automatically lights up again.

When you hold the iPhone in this manner, the voice microphone is in the proper position for it to pick up your voice when you talk. The microphone is located on the bottom of the iPhone housing, so make

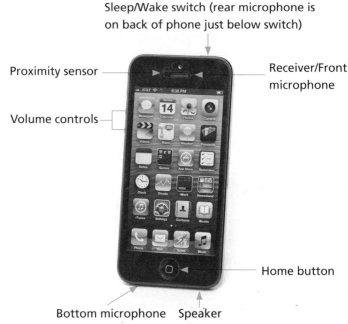

Figure 2-1 *Microphones, speakers, buttons, and sensors on the iPhone*

sure that your fingers don't cover the bottom of the iPhone—otherwise, your voice will be muffled.

Also, while you're holding the phone to your ear, don't block the back of the iPhone housing where the camera is located: a *second* microphone lies between the camera lens and the LED flash (look for a pinhole between the two—that's the second microphone). This second microphone picks up sounds around you (while you're talking or when you shoot videos). The iPhone subtracts the sounds it picks up with this microphone from the sounds it picks up with the bottom microphone so that the person on the other end of your call hears your voice more distinctly.

In short, hold the iPhone by its sides when you are on a call to avoid accidentally covering its microphones.

 A third microphone is inside the opening for the receiver. This microphone is employed when you use the iPhone as a speakerphone.

Dial the iPhone with the Keypad

Now that you know how to hold the iPhone when talking and listening, you need to know how to dial the phone—and, to do that, you also need to know how to tell the iPhone to be a phone! That part is easy, of course: just tap the Phone app icon, shown here.

On a brand-new iPhone, you can find the Phone app at the left end of the *Dock*, the row of four icons located at the bottom of your iPhone's Home screen, as shown in Figure 2-2. You'll learn how to customize your Home screen and how to make use of the Dock in Chapter 5.

When you tap the Phone app icon, the Phone app launches and takes over the screen. At the bottom of this new screen is a row of

Figure 2-2 *The iPhone Home screen with the Phone app at the left end of the Dock*

icons. To use the keypad to dial a phone number, tap the Keypad icon, which opens the iPhone's keypad (Figure 2-3).

 You can make phone calls many different ways with your iPhone. We cover some more of them in Chapter 6.

Next, tap the number you want to call. The numbers you have tapped appear above the keypad. If you tap a wrong digit by mistake, you can use the keypad's backspace key (shown here) to delete it.

Figure 2-3 *The Phone app with the keypad revealed*

Now You Know **What's an App?**

App is short for *application* and is another word for *program*. Apps make your iPhone more than just a mobile phone; in fact, the Phone app is actually a program that Apple developed to make use of all of the telephonic hardware built into your iPhone.

You start an app by tapping its icon on your iPhone's Home screen (shown in Figure 2-2). When an app runs, it takes over the entire iPhone screen; to get back to the Home screen, press the round Home button below the screen on the front of the iPhone.

Apps remember the state they are in when you leave them by pressing the Home button. For example, if the telephone keypad is

(continued)

on the screen in the Phone app when you press the Home button, the next time that you tap the Phone app icon, the keypad appears.

The iPhone comes with a number of presupplied apps, which are described in Chapter 5. In addition, you can obtain many more apps from Apple's App Store, covered in Chapter 11.

Once you have entered the phone number you want to reach, press the bright green Call button near the bottom of the keypad, hold your iPhone's receiver to your ear, and go ahead with your call.

Use Phone Features While on a Call

Although the iPhone screen may be dark and unresponsive to your touch when you hold your iPhone to your ear to talk, it lights up and becomes responsive again as soon as you pull the phone away from your ear while a call is in progress. This is a good thing, because it gives you access to other features you may need to use during a phone call, such as those shown in Figure 2-4.

These features include the following:

- **Mute**   Tap this icon to disable (mute) your iPhone's microphones temporarily so the person at the other end can't hear you. Tap it again to unmute the call.

- **Keypad**   Tap this icon to bring up the keypad again. You can use this, for example, if you are calling an automated system that asks you to enter additional numbers on your phone. ("Press 2 to speak to a customer service representative.")

- **Speaker**   Tap this icon to turn your iPhone into a speakerphone. You can then continue your call with the phone held away from your ear; the sound comes out of the speaker at the bottom of the iPhone instead of the receiver at the top. Tap the icon again to turn off the speakerphone feature.

- **End**   Tap this to end the call.

Figure 2-4 *Phone app features available during a call*

Other capabilities are also available during a call, such as using FaceTime for video chats, adding a call (sometimes called "three-way calling"), and accessing your contacts. Those features are covered later in the book.

Use the Onscreen Keyboard

The original iPhone was one of the first popular mobile phones to offer a touch-sensitive onscreen keyboard, and it still sets the standard. Anytime you are in a situation that requires typing—for example, entering a web address in the iPhone's browser or writing an e-mail—the onscreen keyboard appears (Figure 2-5).

Figure 2-5 *The iPhone's onscreen keyboard*

Basic Typing

To try out the onscreen keyboard, you can use the Notes app (covered in more detail in Chapter 5). The Notes app is on your Home screen, and its icon looks like this:

When you are using an app and want to get back to the Home screen, press the Home button below the iPhone's screen once.

Tap the Notes app icon to launch the app. On the note page that appears, tap anywhere to insert a blinking vertical line—the *insertion point*, or cursor—on the page and bring up the keyboard.

If you don't see a new note page when you launch the Notes app, tap the + button at the top-right of the screen to create a new note:

To use the keyboard to type, just tap its keys. Notice that each character that you type appears briefly above the key. This shows you the key your finger actually tapped. When you lift your finger, the character that you tapped appears in the note.

The fact that a character isn't typed until you lift your finger is an advantage. If you happen to miss your target and tap the wrong key, you can slide your finger to the key you meant to tap before lifting your finger. The key that your finger is on when you lift it is the character that gets typed.

The following keys do something other than type characters when you tap them:

- **Delete/Backspace**   This key, shown here, deletes the character to the left of the insertion point when tapped. Hold down your finger on it and it continues to delete characters. Keep holding it, and it deletes word-by-word instead of character-by-character.

- **Shift**   Tap this key, shown here, and the next character you type appears in uppercase. Tap it twice and it locks (that is, it acts as Caps Lock) so that all subsequent characters are typed in uppercase until you tap the Shift key again to unlock it.

- **Number**   Tap this key, shown here, to see number keys and basic punctuation keys instead of alphabet keys on the keyboard. Also, on the number keyboard, the Shift key is replaced with a Symbol key (not shown): Tap the Symbol key and the keyboard offers additional punctuation and other characters, such as percent sign and square brackets. Tap the ABC key at the bottom-left to return to the alphabet keyboard. In most cases, typing a space also brings back the alphabetic keyboard if either the number or symbol keyboard is displayed.

Other keyboard keys also offer special options. Many normal-looking keys conceal special capabilities. Need accents or other special characters? Hold your finger down on a character key to see any alternative characters that the key offers, as shown next. Then slide your finger to the character you want and lift your finger. Experiment with different letter, number, and punctuation keys to see what they offer; there's a lot of stuff buried under your onscreen keyboard!

Select, Copy, Paste, and Correct Text

As you might expect, you can do more with text on your iPhone than just type it into a note. Any place you can enter text you can also edit it: you can move your insertion point around, you can select text, and you can cut, copy, and paste text.

To move your insertion point, just tap the place in the text where you want it to appear. Don't worry if you don't hit your target exactly: you can hold your finger down on the text to see a magnified view of the current insertion point position and then drag your fingertip to where you want the insertion point to appear, as shown:

To select text, tap twice on any word. The word becomes highlighted, and *grab points* appear at each end of the selection that you can drag with your fingertip to extend or reduce the text selection, as shown next:

 You can also select text by using a *reverse pinch*: Place two fingers on the screen and spread them apart. As you perform this gesture, the text between your two fingertips is selected and highlighted.

When text is selected, you also see a *popover*, also shown in the preceding illustration, with various commands available that you can tap. Although different apps may provide different commands, the following commands are usually available:

- **Cut** Tap this command to remove the selected text and place it in temporary storage on the iPhone's *clipboard*, which always holds the last selection you cut or copied.

- **Copy** Tap this command to put a copy of the selected text on the clipboard while leaving it onscreen.

- **Paste** Tap this command to replace the selected text with the contents of the clipboard. You may also see a Paste command when text is not selected and only an insertion point appears on the screen; in this case, the Paste command inserts the clipboard's contents at the insertion point.

 If you see an arrow symbol at either end of the popover, tap it to see additional commands that you can use.

As you type a word, you may see an *auto-correct* suggestion popover appear. Your iPhone uses an internal dictionary to try to guess the word you are typing and suggests it. Auto-correction suggestions can complete a long word, such as the one shown here, or offer a correction for a typo. To accept the suggestion, tap the space bar, return key, or any punctuation key. To reject the suggestion, tap the *x* on the suggestion popover to dismiss it.

Admit impedim. Love is not love
Which .   lteration
finds, impediment ×

Finally, you can undo any typing or editing you have just performed by shaking the iPhone. When an Undo? button appears, tap it, and the last editing or typing action you performed is undone.

Talk to Siri

The intelligent digital assistant software known as *Siri* was introduced with the iPhone 4S and quickly became that device's most famous, or infamous, feature, spawning endless discussion, advertisements, and parodies. The idea behind Siri (which we'll refer to as "she" because the feature uses a female voice on iPhones configured for American English) is simple: you ask her a question and she answers it, or you ask her to do something for you and she does it.

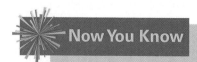

Now You Know | How Siri Learns

Siri is merely software and can misinterpret or fail to understand what you ask (hence, the many Siri parodies you can find on the Internet), but she is remarkably capable software even with her limitations. What's more, Siri can get smarter over time: when you correct Siri, she can learn from your corrections.

Siri requires an Internet connection, either Wi-Fi or high-speed connection through your mobile service provider, because she lives in two places: on your iPhone and on Apple's servers. When you ask a question, the software sends your voice to Apple for interpretation and then consults both the information on your phone—including your contacts and calendars (see Chapter 7), your location, your music and video collection, and so on—as well as the various databases and data analysis systems at Apple that support Siri, to act upon what you asked for. For example, Siri can access weather information for you, find out the scores in a number of popular sporting events, and find movies playing near your current location. She can also open apps for you (for example, say "Open the Notes app"), create reminders, set alarms, and do Internet searches.

As more people use Siri, the software learns to understand more words and phrases and becomes more capable of handling various requests. That's because Apple is constantly analyzing the questions and data that come to its datacenter from Siri (first stripping your data of personally identifying information to protect your privacy) to fine-tune her capabilities. Between the training you give her, the information you make available to her, and the improvements and refinements that Apple continues to make to its analysis systems, you may well find that she becomes smarter and more useful to you as time goes on.

Set Up Siri

Siri should already be set up and ready to use when you first activate your iPhone, but you may want to inspect, and possibly change, the default settings for the feature. You can find those in the Settings app: launch Settings, tap General, swipe down with your finger until you see the Siri heading, and tap it. The Siri settings shown in Figure 2-6 appear.

In addition to turning Siri on or off, you can adjust the following Siri settings:

- **Language**   Tap this to choose the language that Siri will attempt to interpret and will use to respond to you. Not every language spoken by iPhone customers is supported, of course, but Apple continues to add to the languages Siri understands. Some Siri capabilities may also differ among the languages that she does support.

- **Voice Feedback**   Tap this setting to change whether Siri always speaks her responses or speaks only when you have earphones attached or the phone placed against your ear.

- **My Info**   Tap this setting to give Siri your name so she can address you personally. By default, Siri uses the name attached to your card in your Contacts app (see Chapter 7).

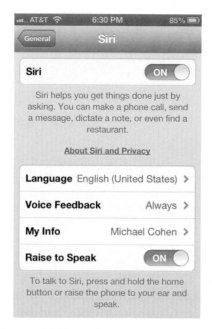

Figure 2-6 *Siri's settings are within the Settings app's General settings.*

- **Raise to Speak**   Turn this on to activate Siri by raising the iPhone to your ear when the screen is on. You can also activate Siri by holding down the Home button below the iPhone screen or by pressing and holding the center button on your EarPods.

See What Siri Can Do

When Siri is activated, the Siri microphone icon appears on your screen, as shown in Figure 2-7. When you speak, the microphone light pulsates in response to your voice so you can tell Siri is listening. Siri automatically detects when you finish speaking, but you can tap the microphone icon to speed things up.

Before you ask Siri your first question, though, you may want to know the kinds of things with which Siri can assist you. Although Apple is continually improving Siri, you can see a list of common questions and requests by tapping the *i* to the right of the text above the

Figure 2-7   *Siri's microphone appears when she's listening.*

microphone, as shown in Figure 2-7. Siri responds with a list similar to the one shown in Figure 2-8. You can tap each of the items in the list to find out more about how Siri helps with that kind of request.

When you ask Siri a question, she may ask for additional information, or, if she is completely baffled, she may suggest a web search, as shown to the right.

Figure 2-8   *Some of the kinds of requests that Siri understands*

Figure 2-9   *Siri can sometimes find answers to some rather obscure questions.*

In most cases, however, Siri can act upon your request or answer your question, even if the question is unusual—it all depends on what Apple has stored in its databases and in the data analysis services that support Siri, as you can see by the answer to the odd question shown in Figure 2-9.

Use Dictation

The last part of learning to type and talk with your iPhone involves both activities: dictation. Your iPhone can handle simple voice dictation tasks so you can reduce your dependence on the onscreen keyboard.

In Figure 2-5, you may have noticed the microphone key next to the space bar on the iPhone keyboard, which is also shown next. This key activates your iPhone's dictation feature. While not part of Siri, the dictation feature is related to her: it, like Siri, uses Apple's data services to analyze and interpret your voice, and it needs an Internet connection to work.

You can use dictation in any situation where the keyboard appears: tap the microphone key, begin speaking when the onscreen microphone appears as shown, and then tap the Done button when you are finished. After a second or two, the words you have spoken appear in the text that you were entering or editing.

Dictation, like Siri, can be remarkably understanding, but it does have its limitations. For one thing, it works only for short bits of speech that are no longer than 30 seconds: don't imagine that you can dictate the Great American Novel at one go. For another thing, it doesn't punctuate for you, so you have to speak your punctuation along with your text. So, for example, if you were Charles Dickens, you would start your novel about the French Revolution by dictating, "It was the best of times comma it was the worst of times comma" and so on. And, of course, you need to pause every so often to have the dictation analysis catch up with you.

For best results, speak slowly and clearly. If the dictation feature is not sure of part of what you dictated, the text appears with a blue underline; tap the underlined text to see alternatives.

3

Receive and Send E-Mail

Electronic mail (e-mail, henceforth) has all but replaced traditional correspondence. Apple provides a very capable e-mail program with your iPhone, bearing the not-very-original name of Mail. In this chapter, we'll show you how to communicate with the mail servers provided by your Internet service provider (ISP), such as Comcast or EarthLink, or other mail service providers, such as Apple for iCloud, your company's Microsoft Exchange service, Yahoo!, Google for Gmail, AOL, or Microsoft for Windows Live Hotmail.

Connect to Your Mail Service Provider

When you initially set up your phone (see Chapter 1), you probably created an e-mail account, either via iCloud with a me.com or icloud .com e-mail address or with another e-mail address that you already possessed. If that's the case, your iPhone already has set up your e-mail account. Unless you're curious or want to let your iPhone know about more e-mail accounts, you can skip to the "Send a Message" section.

Learn How You Get E-mail from a Server

In addition to the corporate and organizational behemoth, Microsoft Exchange, there are two types of e-mail accounts: POP3 (Post Office Protocol, version 3) and IMAP (Internet Message Access Protocol).

POP has been around in one version or another for three-plus decades and is available from many—probably most—ISPs. When you use POP, your mail program downloads e-mail to your device. IMAP, on the other hand, is becoming the standard type of e-mail account: it downloads copies or summaries of your mail to your device but stores your mail on the mail provider's server. This allows users to access their e-mail on the server from multiple locations and devices.

POP is a lot easier and less resource-consumptive for the ISP because the server doesn't need to retain massive amounts of user data or provide for long-term user connections, and, with the local storage of received mail, users don't need to have an Internet connection except for the initial receipt of or the sending of e-mail. On the other hand, in this distributed new world, having all your e-mail accessible on remote storage so that you can reference it from your home computer, your office or classroom computer, or your iPhone or iPad is incredibly convenient. Apple is such a committed IMAP proponent that it eliminated POP access to its iCloud system in the spring of 2012.

Set Up an E-mail Account

As you'll discover, if you haven't already, Settings on the main Home screen is Grand Central Station when it comes to setting up your iPhone hardware and software.

To set up an e-mail account, do the following:

1. Tap Settings on the Home screen. In the Settings screen, slide your finger up until Mail, Contacts, Calendars comes into view (as shown), and then tap it (Figure 3-1). The Mail, Contacts, Calendars screen (Figure 3-2) appears.

Figure 3-1   *The main Settings screen, scrolled to show Mail, Contacts, Calendars*

Figure 3-2   *Mail, Contacts, Calendars settings*

(Note that the author, Dennis, has already set up a number of accounts, and Figure 3-2 shows a populated Accounts list. You will probably see only one or two accounts if you set up iCloud or any other account(s) when setting up your iPhone.)

2. Tap Add Account to open the (you guessed it) Add Account screen.

3. Then do one of the following:

- If you see your mail service on the list, tap it, and, in the screen that slides up, fill in the boxes to set up your e-mail account.

- If your mail provider doesn't appear, tap the Other box to display the screen shown in Figure 3-3. Then tap Add Mail Account to set up an account (either POP or IMAP) through your ISP, fill in the boxes, and tap Next at the upper-right corner of the screen.

Assuming that the information you provided matches what your provider has on file for you, after a short pause you'll see a brief message that your account was verified and it will be added to your list of accounts as shown in Figure 3-2.

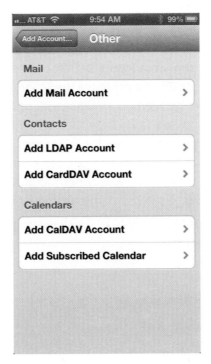

Figure 3-3 *Adding a POP account*

The first setting below the list of accounts is Fetch New Data. This setting determines whether e-mail is "pushed" to your iPhone by servers with that capability, such as iCloud, Microsoft Exchange, and Google. When a mail provider pushes mail to your iPhone, the mail comes to your iPhone almost as soon as it arrives at the server (if, of course, your iPhone has a working Internet connection at that time).

If you turn Push off, which can save on battery usage and cellular data usage (especially if you wait to retrieve mail until you have a Wi-Fi connection), you can specify how often your iPhone checks for new mail. One setting is Manually, in which case the iPhone checks for new messages only when you tell it to do so. Tapping Advanced in the Fetch New Data screen lets you specify Push support or Fetch intervals for each of your accounts, individually.

Establish Other Settings for E-mail

Slide your finger up the Mail, Contacts, Calendars screen to display the
various Mail settings, shown in Figure 3-4. Not all of the Mail settings
fit on one screen if your iPhone predates the iPhone 5, so Figure 3-4 has
more settings than can be seen on an iPhone 4S or earlier screen.

Most of these settings are fairly basic, and sticking with the default
settings provides the proper balance for most users. We describe them
here so you know what they do and so you can change those that aren't
the way you want. In most cases, you either tap an On/Off switch or tap
a more complex setting to see its accompanying screen of options.

- **Show**   Tap this to specify how many messages to display when
  you check your mail.

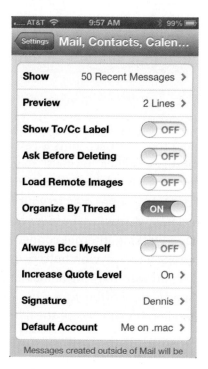

Figure 3-4   *Mail Customization settings*

- **Preview**   Tap this to tell Mail how many lines of each message to display in the preview (this gives you an idea of what's in the message).

- **Show To/Cc Label**   This switch's setting determines whether the addressees are shown on retrieved mail.

- **Ask Before Deleting**   If this switch is On, then deleting a message will invoke an "Are You Sure" dialog.

- **Load Remote Images**   This switch defaults to Off. When On, images referenced in the e-mail, but stored on remote servers, will be retrieved and displayed. (This is a tactical marketing trick designed to give companies information about who actually opens and reads their mail.) Retrieving these images can significantly increase the bandwidth required (and thus your data usage if you're retrieving mail over a cellular connection) and opens a small security hole, because the remote site can track some of your activity.

- **Organize By Thread**   When this switch is On (the default), your replies to an e-mail and follow-ups by others to that e-mail are grouped under a single heading, with a numeric indicator of how many messages are in the thread (sometimes called a "conversation"), as shown in Figure 3-5.

- **Always Bcc Myself**   This switch determines whether Mail will include your account in the Bcc (blind carbon copy) list of addressees.

- **Increase Quote Level**   Turn this switch On to increase the indentation of quoted material in replies and follow-ups. (No, we don't know why Apple chose to use a separate screen with just the switch on it, rather than putting the switch next to the setting.)

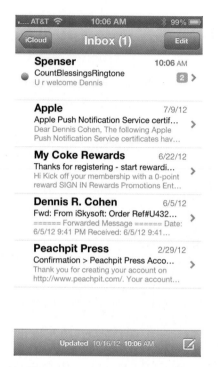

Figure 3-5 *Messages in a thread*

- **Signature** Create a default signature to be placed at the end of messages you send. The default signature is "Sent from my iPhone," which you can leave, replace, or simply delete.

- **Default Account** Specify which mail account that other apps, such as Photos, use when you tell them to create an e-mail message.

Retrieve Your Messages

Once you have set up your e-mail accounts, it's time to use the Mail app to see if you've got mail. Click the Home button to return to the Home screen and tap the Mail icon—by default, it is in the Dock, just to the

About Netiquette

A number of conventions have developed over the decades as to what comprises good "netiquette" (net etiquette). One of these conventions is that signatures should consist of only text and be limited to a maximum of four lines. Another is that you should trim down quoted material to that which is necessary and place your reply to that quoted material beneath it. Yet another is that typing in all caps is considered shouting.

If you happen to communicate with net old-timers and violate these guidelines, they are liable to ignore your message or send back a rude reply. We're old-timers, having started with Internet e-mail back in the 1970s (Dennis) and 1980s (Michael), and though we try to show restraint when receiving blatant violations, we don't always succeed. We get excessively annoyed when we receive a two-screen quoted e-mail and have to try to find the one sentence in that mass of text to which the one-line reply applies.

The rule underlying all the other rules of netiquette: Try to be considerate of others.

right of the Phone icon. The first time you run Mail, you will see the Mailboxes screen, similar to what's seen in Figure 3-6 (the difference being that you'll see your Inboxes rather than ours, and you'll probably have fewer of them, so the Accounts list should be more visible).

The first entry in the Inboxes list, All Inboxes, is a consolidated entry that shows the mail in all your inboxes. This is where you can handle everything at once; however, each account has its own inbox entry that contains only the mail in that account and is useful when you're trying to deal with just one source (say, work), without the distraction of what people and companies are sending to your personal accounts or organizational accounts.

Figure 3-6 *Your Mailboxes and Accounts*

We're going to join the horde of authors, pundits, and other experienced users and recommend that you obtain a free "spam magnet" account (or two), such as one from Yahoo!, Google, or Hotmail. Spam (junk e-mail) is an unfortunate fact of life, and any personal information you make available, such as an e-mail address, in public on the Internet—discussion groups, online forums, Internet newsgroups, and so forth—will be disseminated far and wide to the purveyors of get-rich-quick schemes and male-enhancement products. Use that junk account for your online public dealings to reduce significantly the spam that arrives in your real accounts.

If you want to have Mail check for new messages, press your finger below the word Mailboxes and drag down and release to invoke a manual fetch. If you look while dragging down, you'll see an arrow chasing its tail, as shown next. If you're in the Mailboxes screen or All Inboxes, Mail checks all your accounts. If you have chosen a specific inbox, Mail checks that account.

You can find unread messages by looking for the blue dot to the left of the message preview (see Figure 3-7).

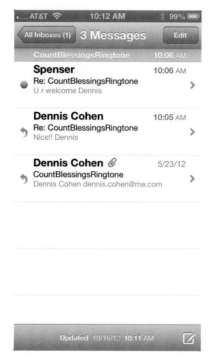

Figure 3-7 *A blue dot indicates an unread message.*

If you want to see the whole message, tap the preview. Your e-mail message appears, similar to the screen shown in Figure 3-8. (Pardon the small print, but that's what happens with a lot of formatted e-mail when viewed on the iPhone screen.) You can zoom-in by double-tapping the screen or placing two fingers on the screen and moving them apart (usually called "unpinching"). Pinching or a subsequent double-tap zooms back out.

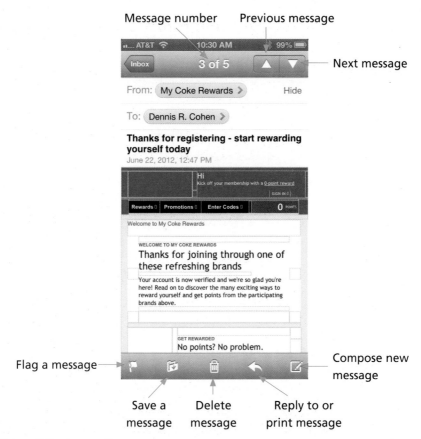

Figure 3-8   *An e-mail message*

At the top of the message screen, Mail tells you how many messages are in the mailbox and which one of that number you're viewing. The two arrows to the right take you to the next (down-arrow) or previous (up-arrow) message. The toolbar along the bottom of the screen allows you to flag a message or mark it as unread; save a message to a mailbox; delete a message (with a cool animation shown on the next page); reply to, forward, or print a message (a menu pops up with your choices); or start a new message (more about these last two in the section "Send a Message").

Send a Message

There are two ways, within the Mail app, to create a message: The first is to reply to a message you've received. The second is to compose a new message.

To reply to a message, tap the curved arrow that points to the left, and you'll be presented with the choices shown here:

Note that if you were the message's sole recipient, Reply All would not be in the list of choices. Tap Reply or Reply All, as desired, and a new message is created with the original message quoted and the sender as addressee and, for a Reply All, the other recipients entered as addressees on the Cc line. The subject is set to "Re: " followed by the subject of the original message, as shown in Figure 3-9.

To create a new message from scratch, tap the icon on the toolbar's far right—the icon that looks like a pen writing on a piece of paper. A blank message is created, as shown in Figure 3-10, leaving it to you to fill in all the blanks—except your signature if you've set one up, which will fill in automatically (mine is simply "Dennis").

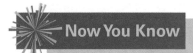

Figure 3-9 *Replying to an e-mail*

Figure 3-10 *A new, blank e-mail message*

Now You Know Addressing an E-mail

Technically, the only thing you absolutely have to fill in is an addressee (To, Cc, or Bcc); however, it is considered poor netiquette to omit a subject—your iPhone will ask you if you're sure about leaving the subject blank—and there isn't much point in sending an empty message. It's also poor form to put your message in the Subject line and leave the message body blank.

You add addressees by using the on-screen keyboard to type in the To, Cc, and Bcc fields, as appropriate. The crucial information for an addressee is his or her e-mail address and, in this digital world, his or her name is not actually necessary. If, however, you do type a name, Mail will search your contacts (more on contacts in Chapter 7) for a match and include the associated e-mail address for you. Alternatively, you can tap the Dictation key on the keyboard and say your contact's name or e-mail address.

Organize Your E-Mail

If you leave all your incoming mail in your Inbox, you'll soon find it difficult to pick a message you want to reference out of the pack. Think of trying to find the one piece of paper you need out of a 6-inch pile in your in-basket. Mail offers a search bar, iOS's Spotlight search, but that will find information only in the Subject, Date, From, To, and Cc fields, not in the message content. Alternatively, you can select a message and move it to a folder (which Mail calls a "mailbox"), just as you do with real mail. Select the message and tap the icon showing an arrow going into a folder. A Mailboxes screen appears, where you can designate in which mailbox you want the message stashed, as demonstrated in Figure 3-11 using a Gmail account.

Tap the mailbox in which you want the selected message stored and you're done.

 There is no way to create new folders on your iPhone; however, you can create new folders on your mail provider's server for some accounts, such as iCloud and Gmail (where they're called "labels").

Figure 3-11   *File a message in a folder*

4

Browse the Web

Until the early 1990s and the development of the World Wide Web, very few people outside of government and academia were aware of the Internet, although bits and pieces of it had been around for more than two decades. Contrary to the myth that grew out of Al Gore's 1999 interview with Wolf Blitzer, the Web that the bulk of the populace equates with "the Internet" was developed at CERN—yes, the same Swiss research facility whose name became a household word because of the book and movie, *The Da Vinci Code*—based on a paper written by Sir Tim Berners-Lee in 1989. Few technical innovations have so quickly caught the public fancy or so rapidly permeated almost all facets of modern life. Today, many major corporations and organizations provide programs to browse the Web: for example, Microsoft has Internet Explorer, Google has Chrome, Mozilla has Firefox, and Apple has Safari.

Meet Mobile Safari

There are obviously some Beach Boys fans among the engineering and marketing folks at Apple. The common terminology for browsing is "surfing the Web," and the lore is that Apple's browser got the name *Safari* from the 1962 hit recording, *Surfin' Safari*.

Connecting to the Internet

You can connect to the Internet via Wi-Fi or a cellular connection, with the usual caveat that using a cellular connection involves nibbling away at your data plan's monthly allotment. So if you're planning to visit media-rich web sites, you should probably wait until you have a Wi-Fi connection, because it will be both faster and less expensive.

Mobile Safari's Screen

Many users rave about how well Safari maximizes the iPhone's screen space and how superior it is to other smartphones' web browsers, and you'll find no argument from us; however, Safari is still limited by the size of the iPhone screen and, as shown in Figure 4-1, if the page you're viewing has a lot of content, you will need to zoom in (using the un-pinch motion or a double-tap) or use a magnifying glass to read that content. To mitigate the situation endemic to all smartphone screens

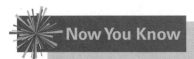 **Now You Know** **Mobile Safari Doesn't Do It All**

The desktop version of Safari, like other "full" web browsers, supports a wide variety of Internet protocols in addition to the *HTTP* (Hypertext Transfer Protocol) and *HTTPS* (secure HTTP) that are encountered when accessing web sites. Two of the other protocols are *file*, which displays a file stored locally, and *FTP* (File Transfer Protocol), which provides the facility to transfer files between remote storage locations and your computer.

iOS doesn't support traditional file management or storage, in which files are under user control. Files in iOS are "owned" by an application, and both storage and access are controlled by the owning application. For example, if you download a non–copy-protected ebook in the MOBI (Mobipocket) format, it can be opened and read in Amazon's Kindle app or in the Stanza app, but not in both (unless you download or sync a duplicate copy of one to the other app).

Figure 4-1 *Safari's presentation can be difficult to read on the iPhone's small screen.*

and browsers, many web sites deploy both a mobile and standard version of their content, so you're going to see a different presentation of those pages on your iPhone than on your computer.

 You can rotate your iPhone to a landscape orientation and see larger text (and a larger keyboard), but this means you'll have to do a lot of scrolling to bring other parts of the page into view.

The top of the Safari screen contains an address box and a search field, so it will be familiar to all who have used a web browser. The navigation buttons (back and forward), which you might expect to see at the left end of this bar, are relocated on the toolbar at the bottom of the screen, making them ever-present when you're browsing. Scrolling down the browser window slides the address box and search field out of view, as shown in the next illustration—a behavior that folks accustomed to computer browsers might find a bit disconcerting at first (believe us, though, that almost everyone becomes quickly accustomed to the change).

Several other buttons are along the bottom toolbar:

- **Action**   (Sometimes called Share) You'll encounter this icon in many apps on your iPhone, which presents a menu when tapped, as shown next. The items in the menu may vary depending on the apps you have installed and other settings.

- **Bookmarks**   Presents the screen shown next. Your bookmarks will obviously be different from mine, but the structure is the same.

    Bookmarks is your access point to bookmarks, browser history, iCloud tabs, and Reading List.

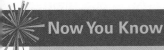 **What About Tabbed Browsing?**

Anyone who has used web browsers during the past six or seven years has become accustomed to tabbed browsing, where you can have multiple web pages open in a single window, each designated by a tab along the top of the window. You can switch to a page by tapping or clicking its tab or close the page by tapping or clicking the tab's close button.

One consequence of the iPhone's smaller screen is that placing tabs along the top of the content area would consume too much valuable screen real estate, especially because it would almost require that the address bar remain static rather than scroll. The compromise Apple provides is the pages screen accessed by tapping the button on the bottom toolbar; this lacks the omnipresence of the tabs but provides thumbnails of the page, which can make finding the one you want easier.

- **Pages** Presents a screen in which you can swipe left or right to switch to another page (similar in functionality to having tabs in a desktop browser) by tapping its thumbnail. Or you can tap the circled X at the upper-left corner of a page thumbnail to close that page, as shown next with the McGraw-Hill Companies page:

Search the Web

Trying to find a page (or selection of pages) containing material you seek on the sprawling behemoth known as the Web is greatly simplified by the availability of search engines that send out automated search tools, known as *spiders* (because they traverse the Web) or *bots* (short for robots), cataloging all they find in the pages they encounter. The first major search engine is still around, and it is the fairly famous Yahoo! engine. Even though Yahoo! is still active and vital, its leadership role was fairly quickly taken over by the search engine whose name became a verb meaning "to search the Web": Google. The third most commonly used search engine is from the folks at Microsoft, and it is named Bing.

Safari gives you access to all three of these search engines through the search box next to the address bar, but the out-of-the-box default engine is Google. If you want to change the default to Yahoo! or Bing, you can tap Settings on your Home screen, scroll down and tap the Safari entry, tap Search Engine in the Safari settings screen, and then tap your preferred search engine.

 You can also go to the search engine's web site (www.google .com, www.yahoo.com, or www.bing.com) and perform your search there rather than via the search box. Or, if you want to use some other search engine you've heard about, you can use it by visiting its web page.

If you tap the search box, the browser window slides to the left, hiding the address bar and expanding the search box's size with a list of recent searches displayed. As you start typing in the search box, possible matches replace the recent searches, as shown at left. If you see what you're looking for, tap it, and Safari will load the search engine's results page (on the right), displaying your "hits." Tap the one you want and Safari loads the page.

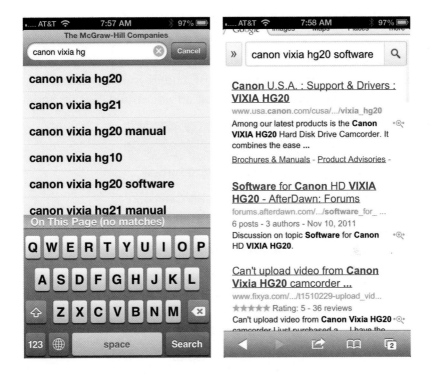

Manage Bookmarks

The Bookmarks button on Safari's toolbar, in addition to being your portal to sites you've marked for revisiting (or frequent visiting), is also where you go to revisit sites that you haven't marked—that is, your browser history.

Access History's Pages

More frequently than most of us would care to admit, we find a need to reference something we've read previously. It might be to obtain or verify some details, it might be to refresh our memory, or it might be to show something we found to another person. In each of these cases, Safari's recording of the pages we visit comes in handy.

Tap the History item in the Bookmarks menu, and you'll see a screen similar to the one shown next. Past dates appear as folders that you can tap to see your browser travelogue for that date. Sites visited on the current day appear at the top of the list, and, if you had visited a number of sites that day, you might see a folder titled "Earlier Today."

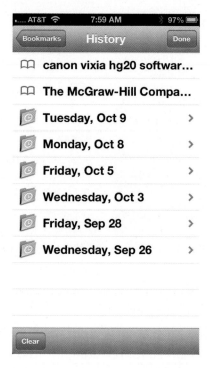

Tap any site in the list and Safari takes you back there, assuming that "there" is still there. The Web is an ever-changing amalgam of sites and pages, with new pages springing into existence and existing pages changing content or even disappearing altogether.

Forget the Past

On occasion, you might want to eliminate the record of where you've been. You've seen in TV shows where the investigators or spies go prowling through someone's browser history to track activity, right? Safari provides a handy Clear button at the bottom left. One quick tap and then an affirmation that you really want your history erased, and, presto, nobody sees where you've been; but you can't go back in time any more either. You can also wipe Safari's cache from the Settings app by tapping the Safari icon and tapping Clear History and Clear Cookies And Data.

Use Reading List

Safari's Reading List feature functions as a snapshot of pages you want to reference or just don't have time to read right now and want to read later.

Reading List is also accessed via the Bookmarks screen (shown earlier in the chapter). What, you might well ask, is the difference between a Reading List entry and a bookmark? The answer is twofold: sometimes nothing, but sometimes a lot. A bookmark is a web address that you revisit, but what you see is the page's current state. A Reading List item is the page at the time you marked it. For pages that don't change, or that change very infrequently, you likely see the same page presentation in either case. For pages that change frequently, such as a newspaper's web site or a page that shows what's playing in local theaters, the content is likely to be quite different from one day (or even hour) to the next. But if you add the page to the Reading List, when you revisit it, you'll see the page as it was when you first added it.

To add the current page to Reading List, tap the Action button, and then tap Add To Reading List.

When you later want to recall the page, tap the Bookmarks button, and then tap Reading List on the screen that appears. The Reading List appears, as shown in Figure 4-2. Two tabs appear near the top of the Reading List screen: All and Unread. As the names imply, All lists all the pages stored in Reading List and Unread lists those pages you've yet to revisit.

Figure 4-2 *The Reading List is where you access content you save for later.*

To remove an item from the Reading List, swipe your finger across its entry on either list and then tap the Delete button—poof, it's gone.

When you're done with Reading List, either tap the Bookmarks button (upper-left) to return to the Bookmarks menu or tap Done (upper-right) to return to whatever page Safari was displaying.

Use Reader

One of the Safari features we like best is Reader. Web pages are crowded with extraneous material such as advertisements, and articles we want to read are presented in snippets, with links to the next and previous pages. Apps such as iBooks have spoiled us with a seamless presentation of the material we want (or need) to read, and Reader offers that same focused presentation to our web browsing.

When Safari recognizes an article or topic on the page you're visiting, a Reader button appears near the right end of the Address box, as shown in Figure 4-3. Tap the Reader button and the article is extracted into a separate screen, as shown in Figure 4-4. The toolbar at the top of Reader's screen includes a button to decrease or increase the font size, the ubiquitous Action button, and a Done button, which you tap when you want to return to Safari's regular display.

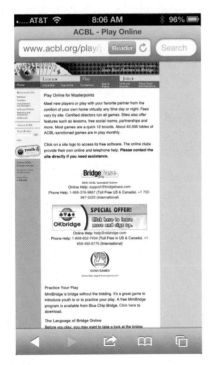

Figure 4-3 *A Reader button appears in the Address box when an article is recognized.*

Play Online for Masterpoints

Meet new players or play with your favorite partner from the comfort of your own home virtually any time day or night. Fees vary by site. Certified directors run all games. Sites also offer features such as lessons, free social rooms, partnerships and more. Most games are a quick 12 boards. About 40,000 tables of ACBL-sanctioned games are in play monthly.

Click on a site logo to access its free software. The online clubs provide their own online and

Figure 4-4 *The Reader screen and its toolbar*

Safari's Not the Only iPhone Browser

Safari is the browser that comes with the iPhone. It is a very good browser, considered by many to be the best desktop browser, and, for mobile devices, it is the browser to which other browsers are compared. That doesn't mean that it is the best browser for everyone. For example, Safari doesn't support viewing content in Adobe Flash format, which is fairly common on the Web.

No two people are alike, and web browsing is, for many, as personal as religion.

Other browsers are available through the App Store—some are standalone and some are integrated into an app. One example of the former is the Chrome browser, a mobile version of Google's Chrome browser for personal computers. An example of integrated browser functionality is Bookman Pro ($1.99), a comic book and PDF reader with a number of interesting features.

If you're curious, visit the App Store and type **Web browser** into the search field; then check out what's available. You will likely find something that interests you.

5

Use the Bundled Apps

A pps are the little (and sometimes not so little) programs you can install on your iPhone to make it almost infinitely versatile. No doubt you have heard the phrase, "There's an app for that." It's a cliché that's true: more than 500,000 apps are available for your iPhone. But right out of the box, your iPhone has a powerful assortment of built-in apps. In this chapter, you'll take a tour of the apps that come bundled with your iPhone 5, and then you'll learn how to arrange them for your convenience.

Meet the Bundled Apps

You've already met a few of the apps that come with your iPhone: the Phone app, the Mail app, the Settings app, and the Safari app. Apple also provides more than 20 other apps as standard accoutrements. You can always count on these apps to be on your phone—you can move them around and organize them, as you'll see later in this chapter, but you can't remove them. These apps provide the basic features that help define your iPhone. Some of them give you access to special hardware features built into your iPhone, such as the internal compass, the camera, and GPS; others provide entertainment features; and others provide basic information access and management capabilities.

You might not use all of the apps that Apple bundles on your iPhone, but we'll bet you will end up using a lot of them. So pick up your iPhone and follow along as we tour your trove of apps.

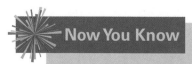

About the Multitasking Bar and Screen Rotation

As you use more and more apps, you might frequently find yourself wanting to switch from one app to another, such as between Safari and Mail. Your iPhone provides a *multitasking bar* that gives you quick access to the apps you've used most recently.

To use the multitasking bar, press the Home button on your iPhone twice, quickly. The screen display slides up, showing a row of app icons at the bottom of the screen. Tap an app icon to switch to that app. You can swipe left and right to move through the complete list of recently used apps.

And here's a bonus: If you swipe left-to-right when you're already at the left end of the icon list, you'll see player controls for your music and other audio apps. You can use these quickly to pause, play, and adjust the volume.

The leftmost control on the multitasking bar is the *orientation lock icon*: tap it to lock or unlock your iPhone's ability to shift automatically between portrait (vertical) and landscape (horizontal) display when you rotate your iPhone. Some apps, such as the Calculator app, provide additional, or alternative, capabilities depending on the screen's rotation, but if portrait orientation is locked, you won't be able to access the capabilities that may be available only in horizontal orientation.

Notes

If you're reading these chapters in order, you've already met this app: you used it in Chapter 2 to make your first forays into the keyboard and dictation. Although Notes is a simple app, it packs in a good deal of convenience and capability—when you have your iPhone with you, it offers an easy-to-use notepad that can contain as many notes as you want. You can use this notepad as you would any paper notepad, to jot down ideas or information that you want to refer to later. You can share your notes with others through e-mail, and if you have an iCloud account on your Mac or PC (see Chapter 10), you can get to your notes there, too. Figure 5-1 shows a typical note (if you're a sonnet aficionado) stored in the Notes app.

At the top of each note, embossed in the brown binding of the notepad (see Figure 5-1), is the note's title. You don't assign your notes titles, though: whatever constitutes the first line of the note *is* the title. It's therefore possible to have more than one note with the same title, just like you can have in a physical notepad. The title is for your convenience, to help you remember what the note contains. Automatically affixed to each note are the date and the time you last edited it.

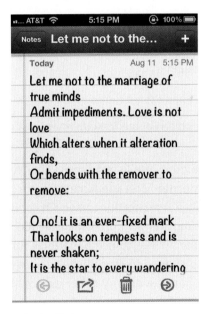

Figure 5-1 *A typical note in the Notes app*

Creating a new note is easy: Tap the + button at the right of the brown binding at the top of the note.

Notes can be longer than a single iPhone screen. Flick up or down to move around in a long note. You can move to the next or previous note in your notepad by tapping the arrow icons at the bottom of the Notes display, as shown next. Tap the Share icon (the rectangle with the curved arrow leaping from it) to send the note to someone via e-mail or to print the note, and you can crumple up the note to throw it away by tapping the Trashcan icon.

In addition to navigating between notes with the arrow icons, you can tap Notes in the binder above the current note (shown in Figure 5-1) to see a list of your notes, as shown here, arranged from most to least recently modified:

You can have more than one list of notes. The Notes app can store notes in any IMAP (Internet Message Access Protocol) mailbox folder you have for any of your mail accounts (see Chapter 3) so you can see your notes on your computer and on any other iOS device that accesses those accounts. You don't have to use a mailbox for your notes, however: you can also choose to store notes on the iPhone itself so they aren't automatically shared with any other device. Tap the Accounts icon in the binder to switch the list of notes to a different account, as shown next:

Accounts	+
All Notes	>
Gmail IMAP	
Notes	>
On My iPhone	
Notes	>
iCloud	
All iCloud	>
Mailboxes galore	>

 To set the account in which newly created notes are stored, open the Settings app, swipe down to Notes, tap it, and then tap Default Account.

Messages

This bundled app sends and receives text messages between phones—and not just phones: it can exchange messages with other devices, too, such as iPads, iPod touches, and Macs. The Messages app can also send and receive multimedia messages containing pictures and videos. We cover this app more fully in Chapter 8.

Photos

Photos is the bundled app you use to see, share, and perform simple editing of photos and other images. The Photos app stores images and videos you've taken with your iPhone's cameras, as well as images that you copy from the web or receive in e-mail. In addition, you can sync images between your iPhone and your photo library on a Mac or a PC with the Photos app. The Photos app stores your images in albums, and you can create albums and move images among them. The Camera Roll album contains the photos you take with your iPhone's cameras.

 You can take a picture of your iPhone screen at any time. Hold down the Sleep/Wake button at the top of the iPhone and press and release the Home button: the screen flashes and you hear a shutter sound. The screen image is stored in the Camera Roll album in the Photos app.

We discuss the various capabilities of the Photos app throughout this book, particularly in Chapters 9 and 10, where we look at syncing, and in Chapters 14 and 15, where we go into detail about how to use the cameras.

Camera

And speaking of cameras, the iPhone has two: one on the front for video chatting and taking self-portrait photos, and one on the back for high-quality photography and videos. This is the app you use to take pictures and shoot videos. We cover how to use the Camera app for photography and videos in Chapters 14 and 15.

Stocks

The Stocks app debuted with the very first iPhone. It provides an almost-current (reports are delayed by 20 minutes) view of the prices of selected stocks, as shown in Figure 5-2.

Tap the price of a stock to cycle between its share price, the company's current market capitalization, and

Figure 5-2 *The venerable Stocks app shows you current stock prices and business news.*

the percentage of change in price from the previous session. The news pane below the list of stocks shows business headlines for the currently selected stock. Tap a headline to open the Safari browser and read the news. Swipe left or right in the news pane to show a graph of the stock's performance over time and to see more details about the stock.

 View the Stocks app in landscape orientation to see a more detailed stock performance graph.

To add stocks to the list, remove them, or arrange the order of the list, tap the *i* icon visible in the bottom-right of Figure 5-2. This reveals the stock information editing view, as shown next:

To add a new stock to the list, tap the + button at the upper-left of the editing view. To remove a stock, tap the red circle to the left of the stock's entry. To move a stock to a different position in the list, hold down your fingertip on the parallel lines to the right of a stock's entry (called the *drag handle*) and drag the entry up or down. Use the buttons at the bottom of the view to choose what statistics the Stocks app displays when you open it. And, of course, when you finish editing the list of stocks, tap Done.

 To retrieve stock information, your iPhone must be connected to the Internet, either through a Wi-Fi or a mobile data connection.

Maps

The Maps app works with the GPS (Global Positioning System) in your iPhone to determine your current location, and it uses the Internet (either via Wi-Fi or mobile data connection) to retrieve maps; therefore, you need an Internet connection to use it. You also need to turn on Location Services in the Settings app if they are currently turned off.

You can use the Maps app to show you maps of where you are, as well as maps of any other locations you enter into its search field, as shown next. Locations can be vague (for example, "Lompoc") or precise (for example, "1221 Avenue of the Americas, New York, New York 10020-1095"). Maps can also provide directions for travel between two locations.

To view directions, tap the bent arrow at the top left of the screen and then enter your starting location and destination in the fields that appear, as shown next. By default, Maps uses your current location for your starting location, but you can change that.

Tap the buttons at the top to switch from driving to walking or public transit instructions. (Note, however, that the first version of Maps in iOS 6 does not actually give you transit instructions but instead takes you to the App Store to find apps that provide transit instructions for your current location.) When you have specified both locations, tap Route to see a choice of routes; tap one of those routes, and then tap Start to get step-by-step instructions for that route.

You can choose to see the maps as graphical images, as satellite views, or as combined satellite and graphic views. For many locations, Maps can also provide current traffic density information along major roadways. Tap the turned up page corner at the bottom right of the Maps screen to see the list of display options, as shown next.

 You can tap the Report A Problem link on the options screen to report problems if the Maps app has provided incorrect information.

Maps can also provide 3D maps and photographic flyover displays of some locations. Tap the 3D or the building icon at the lower-left corner of the map to see a 3D or flyover display, as shown next. (Which icon, if any, appears depends on the displayed location.) To adjust the viewing angle in either the 3D map or normal map, slide two fingers up or down on the map; twist with two fingers to change the orientation of the map on the screen (a compass at the top of the map shows the current orientation relative to north).

To display your current location, tap the arrow icon at the bottom of the map display.

Weather

Like the Maps app, Weather also requires an Internet connection to fetch your local weather information and weather information for other locations that you specify, as well as Location Services to find your local weather automatically. As shown next, the Weather app shows you the day's high and low temperatures, the current conditions, a 12-hour forecast of temperatures and conditions, and a five-day forecast below that.

Swipe left and right to see the weather for other locations that you have specified. To add or remove locations, and to change the order in which they appear when you swipe, tap the *i* icon to see the app's location editing view, shown next:

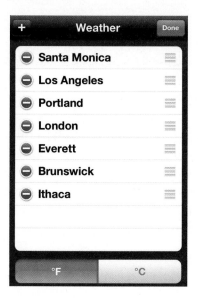

Controls similar to those used in the Stocks app are used to edit the Weather app's locations list: tap the red circle to delete locations, tap the + button to add locations, and use the drag handles to change the order of locations. You can also choose whether to display temperatures in Celsius or Fahrenheit.

Compass

Your iPhone has a built-in electronic compass that can show you which direction you're facing, as shown next:

To use the compass app, hold the iPhone with its top facing away from you and the compass rotates to indicate the current direction. If you have Location Services turned on, the compass can display true north (the direction to the North Pole) as well as magnetic north (the direction to the Magnetic North Pole, which is currently about 4 degrees south of the North Pole, off the northern coast of north-eastern Alaska), and it can show the geographical coordinates of your location. Tap the *i* to change which form of north is displayed.

Magnetic and electrical fields near your iPhone can confuse the compass. If that happens, the Compass app tells you what to do: slowly wave the iPhone around horizontally, twisting its orientation in a figure-8 pattern two or three times to recalibrate it.

Reminders

Use the Reminders app to create checklists of various sorts, such as shopping lists or to-do lists. Figure 5-3 shows a typical list in the Reminders app. To add a reminder to a list, you can tap the + button at the upper-right or tap the first blank line in the list and start typing. To finish adding reminders to the list, tap the Done button that appears at the upper-right.

You can see, specify, and modify details for any reminder by tapping the reminder; the screen shown next appears. Turn on Remind Me On A Day to specify a date and time when you want to be reminded; turn on At A Location to specify that you want to be reminded when you arrive at or leave a specified location (this requires Location Services to be active). To set a reminder's priority, to move it to a different reminder

Figure 5-3 *A list of Reminders*

list, or to add notes to it, tap Show More. Tap Done when you have
finished modifying a reminder's details.

Once you have finished with an item on a list (such as performing the
specified task), tap its checkbox to remove it from the list and move it
to the Completed list, which Reminders automatically creates for you.
To move among your various lists of reminders, swipe left or right.

To see all of your lists, tap the button with the parallel lines at the
upper-left corner of the current list (refer to Figure 5-3). This presents
the Lists screen, shown next.

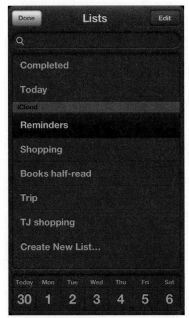

Tap in the search field at the top of the list and start typing to search your reminders for a word or phrase. Tap Create New List to make a new list. To delete lists and arrange their order in the list view, tap the Edit button in the upper-right corner: as with Stocks, Weather, and many other apps, the Reminders app provides delete buttons and drag handles you can use to modify your collection of lists and the order in which they appear. Tap a date on the calendar strip at the bottom of the Lists screen to see any reminders for that date.

The Reminders app has additional settings that you can change in the Settings app. Open Settings, and then flick down until you see Reminders and tap it. You can specify the list in which new reminders will be placed by default. You can also specify how long reminders remain on your lists before they expire and drop off.

 Reminders uses your iCloud account, covered in Chapter 10, to sync your reminders among your other iOS devices, as well as with Macs running OS X 10.8 Mountain Lion or later. You can, for example, create a reminder on an iPhone, modify it on a Mac, and later check it off on an iPad if they all sync with the same iCloud account.

Calendar

This app provides calendars where you can specify various events. You can have work calendars, home calendars, calendars that you share, and calendars that you subscribe to. (For example, you can subscribe to a favorite NFL team calendar that displays the team's game schedule.) You can also sync your calendars between iOS devices and Macs or PCs using your iCloud account. We're not going to say any more about the app here, though, because we cover the Calendar app in depth in Chapter 7.

Clock

The Clock app is not just a simple clock: it can display time for multiple time zones, be used as an alarm clock (with multiple alarms), serve as a stopwatch with lap timer capabilities, and remind you when your laundry is done with its timer capability. The icons at the bottom of the Clock app, shown next, allow you to switch between these features with a tap. Note that all of the Clock functions—alarms, stopwatch, timers—continue to operate even if the app isn't open on your iPhone, so you can, for example, start a timer and then check your stocks or play a game.

The world clock feature, shown next, can show the time for any city you specify (any city, that is, that Apple includes in its very large database of cities). To add a new city, tap the + button at the top right of the screen and then enter the name of a city for which you want a clock—if the city can't be found, pick a nearby city that is in the same time zone. For example, if you live in Santa Monica, California, enter Los Angeles. To arrange the order of clocks displayed, or to remove one, tap the Edit button: you use the same red delete buttons and the same drag handles that you have seen in the Stocks, Weather, and other apps.

You can use the alarm feature as a travel alarm clock, but it is capable of much more. You can create and save multiple alarms and activate or deactivate them. To create a new alarm, first tap Alarm to see your list of alarms (if any) and then tap the + button. Then use the controls shown next to specify when the alarm should go off (flick up and down on the dials in the lower half of the display to set the time), whether it should repeat (you can choose which days of the week the alarm goes off), the sound it plays when it goes off (chosen from your iPhone's ringtones and other sounds), whether you can snooze the alarm or not, and a name for the alarm.

The alarms are listed in order according to the time that they are set to go off, as shown. You can activate or deactivate an alarm by tapping its On/Off switch. To change the settings for an alarm or delete an alarm, tap the Edit button. Then tap the arrow that appears at the right of an alarm to change its settings, or tap the red circle that appears to the left of an alarm to delete it.

The stopwatch feature is straightforward, as shown next. Tap the Start button to start the stopwatch; when you do, the Start button becomes a Stop button and the Reset button becomes a Lap button.

Tap Lap to store intermediate times; the current lap time is shown above the main elapsed time, and previous lap times are shown below the main time display. Tap Stop to stop the stopwatch, and tap Reset to clear the main time and all stored lap times.

The timer feature counts down from the amount of time you set to zero, as shown. When it finishes, the timer plays the sound you specify (tap When Timer Ends to choose a sound); you can also choose to have the iPhone *stop* playing sound when the timer ends—this can be handy, for example, if you are listening to music with the Music app and you want to go to sleep while listening. While the timer is running, you can pause, resume, or cancel the timer countdown.

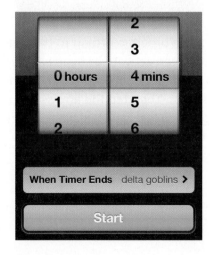

Voice Memos

Voice Memos gives you the ability to record, store, and share audio recordings you make using your iPhone's microphone. The controls are minimal: a red record button at the bottom-left of the screen, and a list button at the bottom-right (as shown next); the rest of the screen is taken up with a big picture of an old-fashioned desk microphone. To make a recording, tap the record button; the record button becomes a pause button and the list button becomes a stop button, which you can tap to end the recording and save it. As you record, the current length of the recording is shown in real time at the top of the app in a red bar. The meter also moves to indicate the current sound level that the iPhone microphone is picking up.

To listen to previous recordings and to share them or delete them, tap the list button. Recordings are listed from newest to oldest. To play a voice memo, tap it and then tap the play button that appears to its left (as shown).

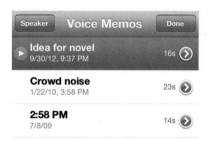

To add a label to the memo (by default, the label is the time of day it was recorded), tap the blue detail button to the right. On the detail screen that appears, you can tap the memo's label to change the label to either a preset label (such as "Idea" or "Interview") or to a custom label. You can also trim the memo's beginning and end. From either the list screen or detail screen, you can share a memo with others, either as an e-mail attachment or as a multimedia message.

 It is considered impolite at least, and illegal in various jurisdictions, to record people without their knowledge or permission. Never record people without letting them know you are doing so and always obtain their consent.

Videos

This app is your built-in video player: movies, music videos, video podcasts, and TV shows that you download, rent, or purchase from Apple are listed in and played using this app. Chapter 12 covers how to stock this app with material and how to use it.

Music

Once upon a time, when the iPhone was brand new, this app was called iPod, and it provided the same audio and video playing capabilities as Apple's hit device of the time. Today, the music and video portions of the app have been separated out, with video playback farmed out to the Videos app. The Music app is where you can store songs and other audio from your iTunes library, as well as music that you purchase directly from Apple. For more about how to use this app, see Chapter 12.

iTunes

The iTunes app confuses some users, because the name leads them to believe that this is the app that they use to play their iTunes music. Not so. The name, actually, is short for "iTunes Store," and this is the app you use to purchase music and video from Apple directly from your iPhone. We describe this app, and how to purchase media with it, in Chapter 12.

App Store

If the bundled apps are not enough for you, you can always get more, and the place to obtain them is Apple's App Store. Use this app to find apps and download them to your iPhone. Chapter 11 discusses how to shop in the App Store.

Calculator

The Calculator app provides the basic functions that any good calculator provides: add, subtract, multiply, and divide keys along with number keys. It also has a memory in which you can store a number and later recall it. But if you view the app in horizontal orientation, the calculator expands, as you can see next. It becomes a scientific calculator with trigonometric and other functions on its extended keypad. What's more, you can tap the 2nd button at the upper-left to bring up additional keys.

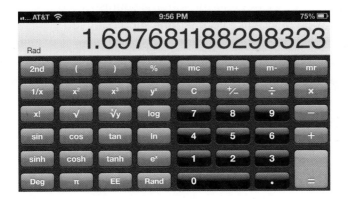

Contacts

As any good mobile phone should, your iPhone stores contact information for the people you call. The Contacts app handles this information, and it can store much more than phone numbers for each contact: e-mail addresses, business and home addresses, nicknames, notes, and on and on. Find out about the Contact app's capabilities in Chapter 7.

Newsstand

When the iPad first came out, publishers began to create digital versions of their magazines and newspapers, some of which were also designed to be read on the iPhone. At first, these were separate apps, but for voracious readers, that quickly became a problem as the number of apps on their iOS devices proliferated like weeds. The explosion of digital print apps led Apple to develop Newsstand, which was designed to collect all of these magazine and newspaper apps in one place and to provide a common way to subscribe to such publications. Chapter 13 describes how to use Newsstand.

Game Center

If you like to play games and think that a sophisticated communication device like your iPhone should let you play games with and communicate with other game players, there's a bundled app for that: Game Center. Lots of game developers have signed up to work with Game Center, so there's a good chance that some of your favorite games work with it. We talk about games and Game Center in Chapter 11.

Passbook App

New to iOS 6, the Passbook app is designed to serve as a holder for various documents (which Apple calls *passes*) from commercial vendors. Such passes include movie tickets, airline boarding passes, and discount coupons, among others. When you purchase something from a vendor that supports Passbook, the passes appear in Passbook, ready to be displayed and scanned by a barcode scanner. For example, if you have a discount card from a coffee-shop chain, that card can appear in Passbook, where you can display it for scanning the next time you visit one of the chain's outlets.

When you open Passbook, it may look very bright: that's because the app ignores the brightness setting on your iPhone so that the passes to be scanned appear clearly when you present them.

The first time you use Passbook, it shows you a list of the sorts of passes it can support, shown here:

The screen includes a link to the App Store so you can obtain other apps that support Passbook. Passes are usually sent to the Passbook app from another app on your iPhone, although some vendors may also send passes as e-mail links or web page links that you can open on your iPhone to have them placed in the Passbook app. Passbook is also location-aware, so it is capable, for example, of displaying a boarding pass automatically when you are at the airport, ready to be scanned. Passbook can even display passes on your iPhone's lock screen so you don't have to unlock your iPhone and open the Passcode app to use it. (You can change this setting in the Settings app's General settings, in the Passcode lock section.)

Arranging Your Apps

You can load apps other than the bundled ones on an iPhone, and, once you've found your way to the App Store (see Chapter 11), you almost certainly will do that. You're not limited to the size of the Home screen you see when you first use your iPhone when you add apps: if there is no room on the Home screen for an app (and a Home screen can hold 20 apps), your iPhone creates an additional Home screen—you can have as many as 11 of them—and puts the app there. But swiping left and right to move through all those Home screens can be wearying. You can reduce the number of Home screens you need by arranging them so that the apps you use the most often are located near each other, by removing apps you rarely if ever use, and by organizing apps into folders.

Arranging and Removing Apps

Jiggling is the key to arranging apps on your Home screens. Touch and hold any app icon on your iPhone until all the icons on the current Home screen begin to jiggle. While the icons are jiggling, hold your fingertip on an icon and drag it elsewhere on the screen. Other icons move out of the way to make room for the icon you're dragging. When you've moved it to where you want it, lift your finger. Note that Home screens store icons in a grid, starting at the top left: you can't drag icons just anywhere on the screen.

 Because the icon grid starts at the upper-left corner of each Home screen, it is the easiest spot to locate. We recommend that you put your Settings app at the upper-left corner of your first Home screen. That way, you can always find it quickly and easily.

You can also move icons from one Home screen to another: just drag an icon to the side of the display to go to the adjacent Home screen, if any.

Jiggling is also the key to removing apps. Although you can't remove the bundled apps, you can remove any apps you obtain from the App Store. Those apps have a circled *X* in their corner when you view them in jiggle mode, as shown next. To remove an app, tap its *X*. Don't worry about removing apps accidentally: you can retrieve them from your iTunes library if you have them synced there (see Chapter 9) or download them again for free from the App Store (see Chapter 11).

Using Folders and Exploiting the Dock

Actually, we misled you: we said that you can have as many as 20 apps on a Home screen, but, in fact, you can have 20 *icons*. What's the difference? Folders. You can collect apps into folders that can hold as many as 16 apps each.

To create a folder, put your iPhone into jiggle mode and drag one app icon onto another: a folder is created automatically, the apps appear in it, and the iPhone even provides a name for it (though you can change it). For example, to rename the folder shown next, just tap the gray *X* to the right of its name field and type a new name. You can also drag app icons out of folders in jiggle mode. (But, no, you can't create folders inside of folders.)

Also at the bottom of every Home screen is the Dock, which remains the same no matter which Home screen is displayed. It can display four icons, and you should put the apps or folders you access most often on it. If the Dock is full, you have to drag an icon off of it before you can drag another one onto it.

Part II

Communicate with Your iPhone

6

Master Advanced
Phone Features

Chapter 2 introduced you to the telephone in your iPhone. iPhone offers more telephony features than the basics we've already covered. There's a speed-dial function called Favorites (you can have up to 50), caller ID ringtones, call-waiting and call-forwarding, conference calling, visual voicemail, and a call history (both the calls made and the calls received). In this chapter, we give you the lowdown on all these features.

 Check out Chapter 2's Siri coverage to see how she can help you make hands-free calls.

Make Favorites

Coincident with Touch-Tone dialing supplanting the rotary dial telephone a half-century ago, a feature called *speed-dialing* started showing up on office phones and then home phones. Limited in scope and usually relegated to a column or row of dedicated buttons, people began to assign frequently called and emergency numbers. Gradually, telephone services began offering up to ten such numbers to be programmed using the asterisk (*) or pound (#) keys on the number keys. This last method is used even today on many basic cell phones.

The iPhone offers you the newest generation of speed-dialing with Favorites. You can specify as many numbers as you want (up to 50) to be favorite phone contacts. In fact, you can even specify favorite FaceTime contacts. (If Apple adds the ability to specify favorite instant messaging contacts, all your iPhone communication channels will be favorite-friendly.)

Create a Favorite

There are two main routes to creating a favorite. The first, and most direct, path is as follows:

1. Tap the Phone app (in the Dock on your Home screen by default).

2. Tap Favorites at the bottom of the screen, as shown next. We already have some Favorites, but if you're starting from scratch, your Favorites list will be empty.

3. Tap the add button (+) at the top of the Favorites screen. The All Contacts list slides into view:

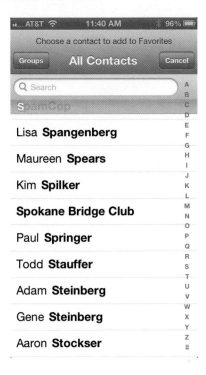

4. Select the contact you want to add. If the contact has only one phone number or only one e-mail address, the dialog shown next appears, asking whether you want to add the number as a Voice Call or FaceTime favorite. (If only an e-mail address exists, it is automatically added as a FaceTime favorite and you're done; skip the next step.) Tap your choice and skip the rest of these steps. Otherwise, if the contact has multiple phone numbers and/or e-mail addresses, you won't see the dialog and you can continue to step 5.

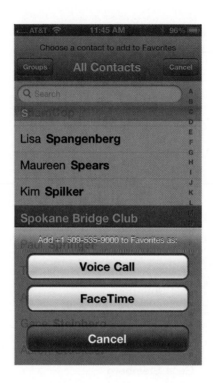

5. The Contact Info for your selected contact appears, as shown next. Tap a phone number and you'll see the dialog shown in step 4. Tap your choice and you're done. Or, if you tap an e-mail address, it is added as a FaceTime favorite.

Use and Manage Favorites

Nothing could be much easier than initiating a phone call or FaceTime session with a favorite. All you do is tap the entry in the Favorites list.

Every item on the Favorites list includes a brief text descriptor that indicates which phone number for the person is on the Favorites contact card—such as home, mobile, iPhone, and so on. If the contact is a FaceTime favorite, a small camera icon appears to the right of the descriptor, as shown in the accompanying image of two entries for Dennis's grandson Bryce: one for Bryce's iPhone number and one for FaceTime.

Delete button   Reorder button

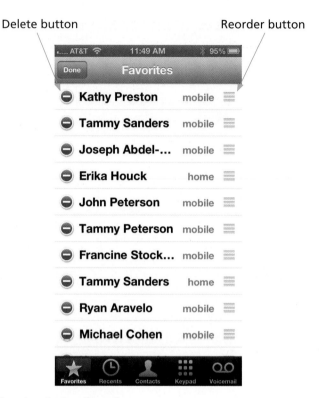

Figure 6-1   *Favorites list in edit mode*

To delete an entry or reorder your Favorites list, start by tapping the Edit button at the upper-left. Your Favorites list launches Edit mode, as shown in Figure 6-1. A minus sign in a red circle appears to the left and an icon of three horizontal lines appears at the far right of each entry. Tap the red circle next to an entry and confirm your intention to remove the entry from the list. To reorder an entry, drag the horizontal lines icon up or down the list and release when it has reached the desired position. Tap the Done button at the upper-left when you're finished adjusting the list.

Assign Ringtones

One of the most loved (and hated) features popularized by cell phones is the ringtone. This audible announcement of a received call tells you who is calling without your having to look. It's extremely popular among (most) cell phone users. In fact, it is so popular that many premade ringtone providers have sprung up across the Internet. Those who don't love the ringtone include people who find the chirping, rapping, singing, or other sounds emanating from the pockets and purses of others to be a distraction or an intrusion in their lives.

Your iPhone comes with a number of ringtones, but you can obtain others or make your own and sync them to your iPhone.

Assigning a ringtone to a contact is a simple process:

1. Tap either the Contacts app or the Contacts icon at the bottom of the iPhone screen.

2. Tap the contact to whom you want to assign a ringtone.

3. Tap the Edit button at the top-right of the screen.

4. Scroll down to where the Ringtone and Text Tone fields are visible, as shown here:

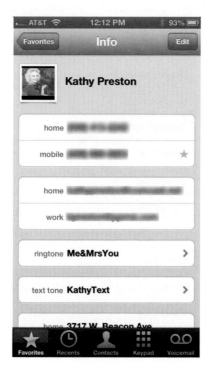

5. Tap Ringtone. (Tapping Text Tone lets you assign a tone to incoming text messages.)

6. In the Ringtone screen that appears (Figure 6-2), you can opt to use the default ringtone (which is established in Settings) or to assign any of the sounds in the Ringtones or Alert Tones lists.

 Your custom ringtones appear at the top of the Ringtones list and are separated from the Apple-supplied ringtones by a slightly thicker gray line, also visible in Figure 6-2.

7. Tap Save (top-right) to return to the Edit screen and then tap Done to finish the assignment.

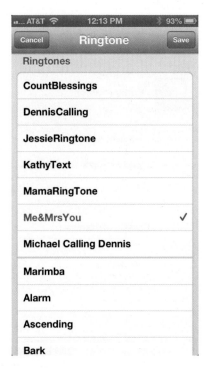

Figure 6-2 *Ringtone assignment central*

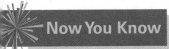

Now You Know   **Adding to Your Ringtones**

At the top of the Ringtone screen (before you scroll down to see the list of available tones) is a button labeled Buy More Tones. Tapping it takes you to the Tones department of the iTunes Store, where you can search for, sample, and purchase additional ringtones. At the time of writing, most of the iTunes ringtones available for sale cost $1.29.

Alternatively, you can search the Internet for iPhone ringtones (and ringtone makers). We recommend using "iPhone ringtone" as your search string for optimal results. As with any such search and purchase over the Internet, you should practice care. Check out the source and read the fine print before providing your personal information, including your credit card number.

Our favorite method, though, is available to Mac users only. Every Mac comes with the GarageBand application. This handy tool lets you create ringtones from any audio files stored in your iTunes Library or any audio file you compose or record using the GarageBand application.

Our commercial favorite is iToner, a handy product from the folks at Ambrosia Software (www.AmbrosiaSW.com), also the maker of Snapz Pro X, our favorite screen and movie capture software and numerous excellent games and utilities.

Use Call Waiting and Call Forwarding

Call waiting and call forwarding are two useful features that, in our opinions, are somewhat underutilized, probably because people either don't know about them or just forget that they are available.

Call waiting gives you the option of ignoring an incoming call when you're in the middle of another phone call (in which case it goes to voicemail), putting your current call on hold and answering the incoming call, or terminating the current call and taking the new call.

If call waiting is turned off, incoming calls go directly to voicemail when you're already involved in a call.

Call forwarding lets you redirect incoming calls to another number. We'll admit to using call forwarding more often on our landlines to transfer calls to our iPhones when we're going out and about, but are expecting a call we don't want to miss; however, you might find reasons to transfer your iPhone calls to another number. (Maybe you want to forward the calls to your spouse when you're playing golf or taking the kids/grandkids to a movie.)

Set Up and Disable Call Waiting

Call waiting is treated differently depending on whether your cell service uses Global System for Mobile (GSM), as AT&T does, or Code Division Multiple Access (CDMA), used by Verizon.

If your cell uses GSM, go to Settings | Phone | Call Waiting and enable or disable call waiting by tapping the switch to ON or OFF, respectively. If your cell uses CDMA, call waiting is automatically on, but you can disable it for an individual call. To disable call waiting (essentially putting a "Do Not Disturb" flag on a call), dial *70 followed by the phone number. You can accomplish this either directly from the keypad or start it on the keypad with *70 and then tap a contact's number in your Contacts list, Recents list, or Favorites.

New in iOS 6 are the Do Not Disturb feature and the ability to defer dealing with a call by either sending a text message or creating a reminder.

Do Not Disturb

If you want to avoid phone calls, or just most calls, you have the ability to set a complete or limited blockade on incoming calls (and text messages). In Settings, you can tap the Do Not Disturb setting to the On position, but for additional control, you'll also have to go to Notifications | Do Not Disturb, where you can schedule a specific period during which you do not want to be disturbed (such as during supper) and exhibit a level of control, allowing some predetermined calls and callers through. For example, you can block anyone but Favorites or a specific group of contacts.

Apple also gives you the option of letting through calls that attempt to reach you a second time within a 3-minute period. The alleged reason is that you might consider multiple attempts in a short period to be a possible emergency situation. (We find that multiple attempts are usually just someone attempting to pester us—your mileage may vary.)

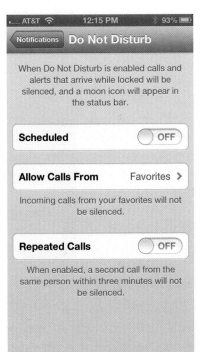

Text Responses and Reminders

Sometimes, when a phone call comes in, you're either busy or just not prepared (or willing) to deal with the call at that time. Your iPhone offers a few options for dealing with the situation.

First, if your iPhone is locked when the call comes in, you can press the Sleep/Wake button once to silence the ring, or press it twice to send the call directly to voicemail. In addition, a small phone icon appears to the right of the Slide To Answer slider. Slide the phone icon upward to reveal the options shown here:

If you tap Reply With Message, you're given the choice of sending some preset messages (Can't talk right now, I'll call you later, I'm on my way, and What's up?) or creating a custom message. The message is sent via iMessage, if available, or via Short Message Service (SMS).

Tapping Remind Me Later gives you one temporal option—to be reminded in one hour—or three location-based reminders (if Location Services is on): when you leave your current location, when you get home, or when you get to work.

 What we'd really like to see added is the ability to ignore a call completely so that it doesn't even get a chance to go to voicemail—a hang-up or disconnect, if you will. That would be a welcome respite with the spate of political campaign calls during election season or a good way to deal with recognizable telemarketers.

Set Up and Disable Call Forwarding

Call forwarding, like call waiting, is turned on and off differently depending upon whether you are on a GSM or CDMA network.

On a GSM network, you turn Call Forwarding on and off by toggling the switch in Settings | Phone | Call Forwarding. If you're turning it on, a Forward To field (shown next) appears, where you either accept the number you used previously, as shown next, or tap it to open the telephone keypad so you can enter the number to which you want your calls forwarded.

 On a GSM network, you'll see a visual indication that Call Forwarding is in effect in the status bar at the top of your iPhone screen—the blue phone and arrow icon seen in the preceding illustration.

On a CDMA network, you turn the feature on by dialing *72, followed by the destination phone number, and then tapping Call. Turn Call Forwarding off by dialing *73 and then tapping Call.

Make Conference Calls

When they want to involve others in their telephone conversations, cell phone users can't just say "pick up the extension," a practice familiar to landline users for many decades. (Of course, with the extension method, others could listen in on our calls—so conference calls have their upside.) Conference calls, also sometimes called three-way calling (although you can have up to five callers at a time on a GSM iPhone), provide a solution and, because the person being invited into the conversation can be located almost anywhere, this feature offers even more convenience. At the time of writing, conference calls require that you be using a GSM network, such as AT&T in the United States.

To originate a conference call, proceed as follows:

1. Make a call.

2. Tap Add Call, and the original call is placed on hold while you call the second conferee.

3. Tap Merge Calls. Now, you and both people you've called are in conference.

4. Repeat steps 2 and 3 to add more people to the conference.

You can speak privately with one person in the conference by tapping Conference and then tapping Private next to the name of person with whom you want to confer. Tap Merge Calls to return to the conference.

To drop a person from the conference, tap Conference and then tap the red hang-up icon next to the name of the person being dropped. Tap End Call to confirm.

If you receive an incoming call from someone you want to add to the conference call, tap the Hold Call + Answer button, and then tap Merge Calls.

Use Voicemail

Voicemail is your service provider's implementation of the old-fashioned answering machine. When you receive a call but you aren't present to answer the phone, you're in the middle of doing something you can't interrupt to answer the phone, or you just don't want to deal with a particular call at the present time (isn't caller ID a marvelous invention?), the caller is redirected to voicemail, where he or she can leave you a message.

Set Up Your Voicemail

The first time you tap Voicemail (the rightmost icon at the bottom of the iPhone screen), iPhone asks you to create a voicemail passcode and record the greeting your callers will hear when they reach your mailbox.

You can choose to use your provider's default greeting—the ubiquitous, "You have reached the voice mailbox of …" by tapping Default, or you can record your own greeting by tapping Custom, and then Record, and speaking your greeting, followed by a tap of the Stop button.

Tap Play to review how your greeting sounds. If you're satisfied, tap Save; otherwise, tap Record again and repeat the process until you are satisfied; then tap Save.

You can change your voicemail passcode by tapping Settings | Phone | Change Voicemail Password and following the on-screen prompts. Alternatively, you can tap the Greeting button on the Voicemail screen, as described in the next section, and proceed from there.

Check Your Voicemail

When you have unheard messages in your voice mailbox, the Phone app places a numeric badge on the Voicemail icon to indicate the number of unheard messages.

Tap Voicemail to see a list of your messages, as shown in Figure 6-3. Each call is indicated by whatever caller ID information was available and the time of the call. Calls you haven't listened to are designated by

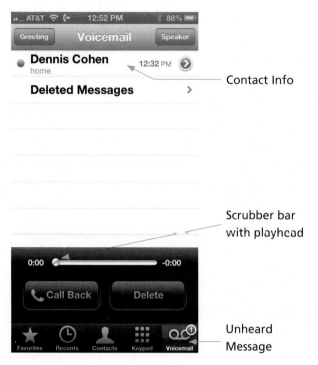

Contact Info

Scrubber bar
with playhead

Unheard
Message

Figure 6-3 *The Voicemail screen*

a blue dot to the left of the caller indicator, as shown at the top of the screen in the figure.

Tapping the Greeting button at the upper-left corner takes you to the Voicemail Greeting screen , where you can alter your greeting (or set one up if you opted for the default during your initial setup).

Tap the blue and white arrow to the right of an item to see all the information that your carrier can provide for numbers that aren't already in your Contacts, or to see information stored on your info card for those that are included.

To play a message, tap it. If the Speaker button at the upper-right corner is highlighted, your message will play through the iPhone's speaker; otherwise, hold the phone up to your ear to listen to the voicemail, just as if you were taking a call.

If you have a Bluetooth audio device active, the Speaker button changes to an Input button, and tapping it lets you specify whether the phone, the speaker, or your Bluetooth device provides the audio.

When a message is playing, a scrubber bar appears and you can drag the playhead back and forth to skip to different parts of the message.

To delete a voicemail, tap the entry, and then tap the Delete button. Or you can swipe across the message and then tap Delete to clear that message out of your carrier's system. Tap Deleted Messages to display all the voicemails you've deleted but not cleared from your carrier's system or that your carrier hasn't cleared in its cleanup of old messages.

We don't have a definitive answer as to how long your carrier will let old messages "hang around," but at the time we're writing this, Dennis has a few messages from nine months back still lurking (which spurs him to take a short break from writing and clear the detritus).

In typical iOS fashion, in the Deleted Messages list, you can tap a message and then tap Undelete to return the message to your Voicemail list. Finally, you can tap the Clear All button and wipe out all your deleted messages.

Pick and Choose the Voicemail You Want to Hear

Apple calls the iPhone voicemail feature *visual voicemail*, because, unlike with traditional voicemail systems, you aren't dealing with a sequential, tape-like system. You can see all the available calls (that's the "visual" part) and select which ones you want and the order in which you want them. The *scrubber bar* is another visual feature; you can drag its playhead to a specific time code within the message to start listening—no need for guesstimating with a fast-forward and rewind feature.

Manage the Recents List

If you've watched cop shows on TV, particularly a series like *Law &
Order*, you've encountered detectives asking for the "lugs" on a phone
number—in other words, the history of calls to and from that number.
The Phone app's Recents list shows that history, unless you make
modifications to it by deleting some or all of the entries. Not only does
it show a history of all calls made and received, but it also lists all the
Missed calls—those that weren't answered and didn't go to voicemail—
in red, as shown next:

You can tap a call in the Recents list to call the number. Tap the little
arrow to the right of the call to get caller information from your
Contacts list or, lacking an entry for that number in Contacts, you'll see
any information that your carrier can make available through caller ID.

Tapping the All and Missed buttons at the top of the screen lets you switch between viewing all calls in your history or just the calls that you didn't answer.

If you see a call in the list from someone you want to add to your Contacts, tap the arrow to the right and, in the Info screen that appears, scroll down to tap either Create New Contact or Add to Existing Contact (useful when you find a new phone number, such as a work or cell number, for someone already included in your Contacts).

Also available in the Info screen are buttons to call the number, initiate a FaceTime conversation with the number, or send a message (SMS, MMS [Multimedia Messaging Service], or iMessage) to the number. There's also a Share Contact button that lets you send an e-mail or message to any contact with this call's contact info attached.

If you tap the Edit button at the top-right corner of the Recents list screen, a Clear button appears at the top-left corner. Tap the Clear button to remove all entries from the list. To remove individual entries, tap the minus sign in a red circle to the left of the entry (and shown next), and then tap the Delete button that appears on the right. This is really handy for eliminating trash calls, such as wrong numbers and solicitations by charities or political campaigns that are exempt from the federal Do Not Call Registry restrictions. (Dennis tries very hard to avoid voting for any candidate or cause that disturbs his peace and chews into his cellular minutes by calling his cell phone.)

Emergency Call Feature

When your iPhone (or any iPhone you pick up) is locked and requires a passcode to unlock it, you can still make an emergency call. Tap the Emergency Call button at the bottom of the Enter Passcode screen. A keypad will appear, as shown next, so you can make the urgent call.

7

Use Contacts and Calendars

Almost since the first mobile phones hit the market, they have included some sort of contact list capability for storing phone numbers and names so you wouldn't have to fumble with a separate address book to make a call on the go. And soon after that, mobile phones began to offer rudimentary calendar features, too, so you could keep track of your day's appointments. The iPhone offers these de rigueur features with bells and whistles added (literally—you can have calendar alerts that play bells, whistles, or any other tone stored on your iPhone).

In this chapter, we'll tell you how to create and use your iPhone's contact list for sending mail, making phone calls, and even getting directions. We'll also explain how to create calendar events, set alerts to remind you of upcoming events, use multiple calendars for different purposes, and subscribe to calendars from other sources (such as your kids' soccer league schedules).

Use the Contacts App

You use the Contacts app to store and view information about the people, businesses, and organizations with whom you interact. For each entry, you can store a wealth of information: name, telephone numbers, e-mail addresses, mailing addresses, birthdays, nicknames, notes, and more, as shown next. You can access this information as you're using other apps on your iPhone; for example, you can retrieve a contact's phone numbers in the Phone app to dial a number or use a contact's e-mail address in the Mail app to send a message.

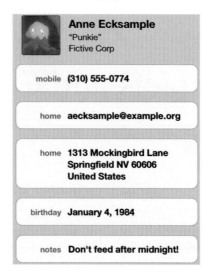

You can add contact entries to your iPhone by typing them in, but you can also add them from your computer and from online accounts, such as your Gmail, iCloud, Yahoo!, Facebook, or AOL account. In fact, in the Settings app, mail, contacts, and calendars are grouped together, as you can see.

Turn on Contacts in an Account

If you followed the instructions in Chapter 3 to set up an e-mail account, and if the account was one of the branded account types—iCloud, Exchange, Gmail, Yahoo!, AOL, or Hotmail—then it may have a contact list (sometimes called an *address book*) associated with it. To add those contacts to your Contacts app, do the following:

1. Open Settings and tap Mail, Contacts, Calendars.

2. Under Accounts, tap the account from which you want to get contacts.

3. On that account's screen, turn on Contacts, as shown:

If you set up a different sort of account, you have the option of getting contact information from it if the account supports either Lightweight Directory Access Protocol (LDAP) or CardDAV contact information. Your account provider can tell you which one it uses and the appropriate settings you need to specify.

To use an LDAP or a CardDAV account for contacts, do the following:

1. In the Settings app, tap Mail, Contacts, Calendars.

2. Under Accounts, tap Add Account, and then flick down and tap Other.

3. On the Other screen, tap either Add LDAP Account or Add CardDAV Account, as shown:

4. On the screens that follow, enter the required information (supplied to you by your account administrator).

When you add an account to your Contacts, that information is regularly synced with your iPhone when you have an Internet connection. That means if you change the contact information on your iPhone, your changes sync back to the account over the Internet; similarly, if you change some contact information on your computer, the changes appear on your iPhone.

Now You Know **vCards, CardDAV, LDAP, and Contacts**

What's that alphabet soup all about? The burden of history: methods for storing and retrieving contact information to use with computer systems for various purposes have been invented and reinvented several times. Eventually, a few standard methods were devised, and the iPhone makes use of them.

- **vCard**   This is a standard for storing a single contact. For example, programs such as OS X's Contacts app (known as Address Book in earlier versions of the Mac OS) can export a contact as a vCard, which can be attached to an e-mail message. If you receive a vCard attachment on your iPhone, you can tap it in Mail to add that contact and its associated information to your Contacts app.

- **CardDAV**   This is a standard used to store contact information on a server. Information on a CardDAV server is usually stored as collections of vCards. Your iPhone can access an account on a CardDAV server to sync contact information with your iPhone.

- **LDAP**   The Lightweight Directory Access Protocol is often used on corporate e-mail servers for storing contact information (among other things). As with CardDAV, you can set up your iPhone to sync contact information with LDAP servers.

You need to know these things only if you have an account that uses them. Don't worry about the details of how they work, though; that's your system administrator's problem.

You can use contacts from several different accounts at the same time. For example, you can see contacts from both an iCloud account and an Exchange account at the same time. To see contacts from just one account, tap the Groups button to choose the account to view.

To see the contacts from all of your accounts at once, tap All Contacts on the Groups screen. If you have the same contact with the same name listed in several accounts, the contact appears only once in your contacts list on your iPhone when you view All Contacts, and the information from all of the accounts is combined on that contact's entry; in addition, "Unified Info" appears at the top of the screen when that contact is displayed. If you make a change to the contact's information on your iPhone, the changes are synced to each of the accounts that provide that contact. You don't have to keep track of which information came from which account; your iPhone handles that for you.

Some types of accounts allow you to arrange your contacts into groups. For example, on your Mac or PC, you may create a group for work contacts and another group for personal friends. The Groups screen in the Contacts app shows any such groups that you have created in the accounts you add. Although you cannot make new groups in the Contacts app, you can use the ones that you make elsewhere.

 For some types of accounts, the contact information may be read-only—that is, you can bring the information into your iPhone, but you can't add any contacts to that account, nor can you change them. For these accounts, you won't see the + button for adding new contacts.

Create, Edit, and Delete a Contact

To create a new contact, do the following:

1. In the Contacts app, tap the white + at the upper-right corner of the contacts list, as shown:

2. In the New Contact page that appears (shown next), tap and fill out the fields for which you want to supply information. Some information you enter by typing; you choose other information from a list of items. For example, when you tap the Add Photo field, you can take a photo or choose an image from your iPhone's photo collection.

3. Tap Done when you have finished.

 Flick down to the bottom of the page to see the Add Field button. Tap it to see a list of additional fields you can add to a contact, such as a Twitter handle or a Notes field. Tap one of the fields to add it to your contact.

Follow these steps to edit an existing contact's information:

1. In the contacts list, tap the contact you want to edit.

2. At the top-right of the contact's page, tap Edit. The fields become editable, as shown:

3. Do any of the following:

   - To edit information in a field, tap it.
   - To delete a field, tap the red circled – to its left.
   - To add a new field, tap a field with a green circled + to its left.

4. Tap Done when you have finished editing.

 To move quickly through your list of contacts, tap a letter to the right of the list, as shown, or tap the search field and type in a contact name.

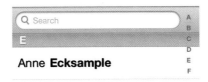

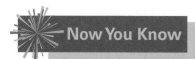 **Default Contacts Account**

If more than one account syncs contacts with your iPhone, you might wonder which account receives new contacts you create on your iPhone. In fact, new contacts are added to the iPhone's default contacts account. You can specify the default contacts account like this:

1. Open the Settings app and tap Mail, Contacts, Calendars.

2. Flick down to the Contacts section on that page and tap Default Account. (This option doesn't appear unless you have multiple accounts supplying contacts to your Contacts app.)

3. Choose the account you want to store new contacts you create on your iPhone.

To delete a contact, follow these steps:

1. In the contacts list, tap the contact name.

2. Tap Edit at the top of that contact's page.

3. Flick to the bottom of the contact information and tap Delete Contact.

Use Contacts with Mail

Your iPhone's Mail app works with your Contacts app so you seldom have to type a complete e-mail address by hand. Mail can fetch e-mail addresses directly from your contacts list.

One way to address your mail to a contact is to begin typing the contact's name or address in the To, CC, or BCC part of the message. As you type, Mail shows you a list of contacts that match what you have typed so far. If the contact appears on the list (which may quickly narrow down to one item, as shown), tap it to add that contact's e-mail address.

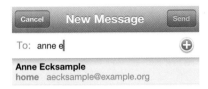

Another way is to ask Mail to show you your contacts by first tapping an address field (To, CC, or BCC) and then tapping the blue circled + that appears at the right of the field. The All Contacts list appears, as shown. Tap a contact to add that contact's address to the address field; if the contact has more than one address, you have an opportunity to choose which address is used.

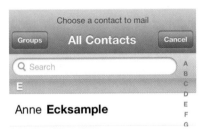

Make Calls with Contacts

As mentioned at the beginning of this chapter, using a contact list to help you make phone calls is one of the oldest mobile phone features. Here's how you use contacts to make phone calls on your iPhone:

1. Open the Phone app.

2. At the bottom of the screen, tap Contacts, as shown. Your list of contacts appears.

3. Tap the contact you want to call, and then, when the contact's information appears, tap the phone number you want to use; some contacts may have more than one.

 You can also make calls from within the Contacts app: Open a contact entry and tap the number on it that you want to call. The Contacts app opens the Phone app and dials the number.

Get Directions

The Maps app and the Contacts app also have a close working relationship. For example, if you tap an address on a contact's information page, the Maps app opens to show you where the address is located, as shown next:

You can also use this feature to get directions to that contact's address. At the upper-left corner of the Maps screen, tap the bent

Figure 7-1   *Choose start and end locations for directions.*

arrow. The Maps app provides two fields at the top of the screen, as shown in Figure 7-1: a Start field with your contact's address, and an End field that you can tap and fill out. Note that when you have Location Services turned on, the starting location is automatically filled in with your current location, as it is in Figure 7-1. As you type in either field, Maps suggests locations that you have visited, contact addresses, and locations it knows about to match what you type.

You can choose what kinds of directions you get by clicking the icons above the addresses: driving directions, walking directions, and public transportation directions. In the first version of Maps for iOS 6, however, walking directions are not available in many areas, and public transportation directions take you to the App Store to get an app that provides such information.

To swap the starting and ending location, tap the swap button at the left of the address fields; it's labeled with a double-pointed, double-bent arrow (visible in Figure 7-1).

Use the Calendar App

Early calendar features on mobile phones were basic: they presented a list of uneditable events and times, usually transferred by ˜necting the phone (via a cable!) to a computer running a syncing handled calendar data stored on the computer. The Cale your iPhone, however, can obtain its calendar events w Internet from all sorts of different calendar sources, ir example, iCloud, Exchange, and Gmail accounts. The

events from multiple calendars at the same time: for example, the events on a Work calendar from Exchange and from both a Home and Vacation calendar from iCloud.

Turn on Calendars in an Account

As with contacts, if you followed the instructions in Chapter 3 to set up an e-mail account, that account may have calendars associated with it. To add an account's calendars to the Contacts app, follow these steps:

1. Open Settings and tap Mail, Contacts, Calendars.

2. Under Accounts, tap the account from which you want to get calendars.

3. If that account has one or more calendars associated with it, the account's screen displays a Calendars switch; turn on the switch, as shown:

You can also get calendars from a calendar account on a server that uses a protocol known as CalDAV. Your account provider can tell you if it provides CalDAV accounts.

To use a CalDAV account for calendars, do this:

1. In the Settings app, tap Mail, Contacts, Calendars.

2. Under Accounts, tap Add Account, and then tap Other.

3. On the Other screen, tap Add CalDAV Account, as shown:

4. On the following screens, enter the required information.

When you add a calendar account to your iPhone, the iPhone syncs that information regularly between the server and your iPhone. So if you create a new event on a calendar, that information is also sent to the server where it is available to other calendar programs that use the same calendar account.

Make and Edit Calendar Events

In calendar-speak, an *event* is an item on the calendar that has a beginning date (and optionally a time), an ending date (and time), and a title. Events on your iPhone calendars can also include other information, such as notes, if the event indicates whether you are busy during the event or free (useful for those who like to avoid double-booking appointments), whether an alert should be given when the event is approaching, and, if so, how long before the event the alert should happen.

Here's what you do to create a calendar event:

1. Open the Calendar app and, at the upper-right corner of the current calendar page, tap the white + button:

2. On the Add Event screen, as shown, type in a title for your event, and, optionally, a location (such as an address or meeting room number).

3. Tap the panel that shows the start and end times and then, on the Start & End screen that appears, use the dials that appear at the bottom of the screen, as shown, to choose a date and (optionally) starting time for the event (flick the dials up or down to turn them). Tap the Ends field and, using the dials, set an end date and time. For events that last full days, set the All-day switch to On.

4. At the top of the Start & End screen, tap Done. Then tap additional fields on the Add Event screen to set them. These fields include the following:

- **Repeat**   Tap this field to set whether an event recurs, and, if so, the amount of time between occurrences.

- **Invitees**   Tap this field to send e-mail invitations to the event to others. You have access to your contacts list on the Add Invitees page.

- **Alert**   Use this to specify whether an alert should be issued as the event approaches. You can choose how long before the event the alert is issued. Alerts appear as a message on your iPhone screen accompanied by the sound you have chosen in the Settings app as your Calendar Alert sound. After you have set one alert for an event, you have the option of setting a second alert as well.

- **Calendar**   If you have more than one calendar on your iPhone, tap this to choose the calendar on which to place the event.

- **URL**   If a web address is associated with the event, you can enter it here.

- **Notes**   Use this field to add any details about the event not included in the other event fields.

5. When you finish making your settings, at the top of the Add Event screen, tap Done.

Editing an existing event is much like creating a new event:

1. On a calendar, tap an event you want to edit.

2. On the Event Details page that appears, tap Edit. You'll see the same fields on the Edit Event page that appear on the Add Event page.

3. Make your changes and tap Done.

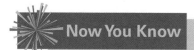

Now You Know | **Calendar Defaults and Calendar Alert Sounds**

In the Mail, Contacts, Calendars settings page in the Settings app, you can set a number of calendar-related options in the Calendar section:

- **New Invitation Alerts**   Turn this on to receive alerts if someone sends you a calendar invitation.

- **Time Zone Support**   Turn this on and specify a city to have all events on your calendar adjusted for that time zone. Turn it off to have the Calendars app use the time zone for your current location.

- **Sync**   Use this to specify how far back events synced from your calendar accounts go on your iPhone. Your calendar account may store events going back for years, but adjusting this setting can help you keep old events from cluttering your iPhone's copy of your calendars.

- **Default Alert Times**   You can set whether events automatically issue alerts, and if so, how long before the event those alerts occur. You can specify alert times for three different kinds of alerts: birthdays (the Calendar app knows about these from the optional Birthday field in the Contacts app), regular events, and all-day events.

- **Default Calendar**   If you have more than one calendar in the Calendars app, use this to set the calendar on which new events are stored (although, as you have just seen, you can change this at any time).

You can also set the sound that plays when a calendar alert is issued. In the Settings app, tap Sounds, and flick down the page to Calendar Alerts; tap it and choose a sound.

Use Multiple Calendars

With the Calendars app you can have more than one calendar in an account, and more than one account. When you have more than one calendar, a Calendars button appears at the top of the calendar page (the exact title of this page indicates the number of calendars for which it shows events—for example, All Calendars, 5 Calendars, or No Calendars). Tap the Calendar button to see the list of your calendars, the accounts to which they belong, and whether or not the events from a calendar are shown on the calendar page (see Figure 7-2).

To keep events from a specific calendar from appearing on the calendar page, tap the calendar name to turn off the checkmark; tap it again to bring the checkmark back.

To make changes to a calendar, tap the blue and white arrow button at the right of the calendar's name. You can change the color that is associated with its events, change its name, or delete the calendar. You can also add new calendars to an account from your iPhone. You can also delete calendars from an account, but heed the following warning.

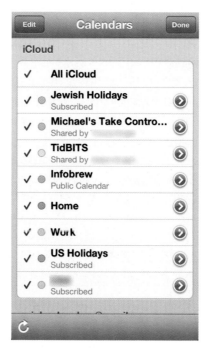

Figure 7-2   *A list of calendars*

 Deleting a calendar on your iPhone can also delete it from the account to which it belongs! Exercise caution when using this capability.

Subscribe to Calendars

In addition to the calendars you directly control in your accounts, you can also view calendars to which you subscribe in the Calendars app. Subscribed calendars are created by someone other than you; you can view, but not change, the events on subscribed calendars. Subscribed calendars are useful for events that many people share, such as lists of holidays or sporting event schedules; many professional sporting teams provide calendars to which you can subscribe with your iPhone.

The website at http://icalshare.com/ offers a wide variety of calendars that you can subscribe to.

Two kinds of subscribed calendars can appear on your iPhone. One kind, three examples of which are shown in Figure 7-2, are calendars to which you subscribe using a calendar program on your computer and that you add to the calendars that you sync between your computer and your iPhone. For example, Michael subscribed on his Mac to the three subscribed calendars visible in Figure 7-2, and he added them to his collection of iCloud calendars on his computer; that's why they show up in the iCloud calendars list on his iPhone. If he were to delete these calendars on his iPhone, they would be deleted in his iCloud account and vanish from all his devices that use that iCloud account! (Refer to the warning a little earlier in this chapter.)

The second kind of subscribed calendar consists of calendars to which you subscribe *directly* on your iPhone. These subscribed calendars are noted on the Calendars screen in their own section, such as the Infobrew calendar shown next. To subscribe to a calendar directly on your iPhone, you usually tap a subscription link in an e-mail or on a web page; then your iPhone asks you whether you want to subscribe. Once you confirm, that calendar appears in the Subscribed section of the Calendars page.

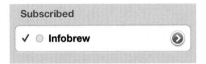

You can safely delete a calendar to which you have subscribed directly on your iPhone. Unlike calendars that you create, or those that are synced with another account such as your iCloud account, deleting this kind of a subscribed calendar is perfectly safe, because it is removed only from your iPhone, and not anywhere else. To delete such a subscribed calendar, follow these steps:

1. Go to the Mail, Contacts, Calendars page in the Settings app. Subscribed Calendars appears in the list of Accounts if you have subscribed calendars.

2. Tap Subscribed Calendars, and then tap the calendar you want to remove. You'll see the calendar's detailed server information and, at the bottom of the page, a Delete Account button.

3. Tap Delete Account to remove the calendar and its events from your iPhone.

 You can turn off the Accounts switch at the top of a subscribed calendar's page in Mail, Contacts, Calendars to remove it from your Calendar app. Later, if you like, you can turn it back on so that it again appears in the Calendars app.

8

Communicate with Text and Images

Yου see them everywhere, their eyes focused on their mobile phones as their fingers fly across the keyboards. If you haven't already guessed, these people are *texting*: using their phones to send messages to other people's phones. These messages aren't full-length e-mails but short utterances of a dozen words or so at a time. It's like passing notes in class, but with a phone instead of paper. In this chapter we will explore the various messaging options available for you to use with your iPhone, including Apple's iMessage service. We'll also provide a brief introduction to the world of social networking.

Use Messages

If you already use text messaging, you don't need us to explain it to you. If you don't use it, the concept is simple: enter a phone number (or your contact's name, and the smartphone will automatically fill in the number), use your phone's keyboard to type a short message, and tap a send button. Voilà! The message appears on the recipient's phone. Text messaging is not a medium for writing the Great American Novel or even the Great American Haiku. You use it when you want to send a short, quick note to someone else. As you might expect, your iPhone not only provides this standard mobile phone capability, known as SMS

(Short Message Service), but also expands upon it with its iCloud-based iMessages. We cover both in this chapter.

Send and Receive Texts with SMS

Although SMS is a phone feature, you don't use the Phone app to send or receive SMS messages. Instead, you use the Messages app. This app not only sends and receives SMS messages, but it also maintains a record of sent and received messages so you can review older texts; you can also edit the stored texts to delete those that are no longer of interest to you.

Now You Know   What is SMS?

The Short Message Service used with mobile phones piggybacks on the standard signal paths that mobile phone networks use to control traffic. When a mobile phone is not using these paths for control purposes, it can be used to carry short textual messages. And short means short: to fit into the control signal format, a text message is limited to 160 characters. If you want to send a longer message, it must be broken up into multiple SMS messages, each no longer than the 160-character limit.

Because SMS is a standard, you can send SMS text messages between different models of mobile phones and between phones that use different carriers. All you need at each end is a phone with SMS capability connected to a mobile phone network.

Most mobile phone plans provided by the major services offer text message capability as an add-on service; for example, a plan may include a limited number of SMS texts sent or received per billing cycle. (That's right: both the sender and the recipient of a text message are charged for each message.) They also offer pay-per-use SMS service, with which you pay for each message sent or received. Typically, pay-per-use SMS service costs between 10 cents and 20 cents per text message.

Here is how you can send an SMS text to a new recipient:

1. On your Home screen, tap Messages. On the screen that appears, you see a list of any previous SMS text message conversations, as shown; if you have never sent or received a text message, the list is empty.

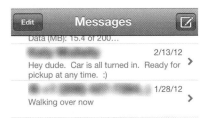

2. Tap the Compose button at the upper right. A New Message screen like the one shown next appears.

3. In the To section, type the phone number of the recipient of the message. Alternately, tap the blue-circled + to see your contacts list, tap a contact, and then tap the contact's mobile phone number.

4. In the text entry field, as shown, type your message and then tap Send. Notice that as you type, the number of characters in your message appears to the right of the text entry field.

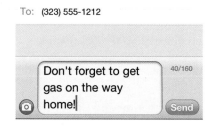

Usually, the text message is sent within seconds, although it may take longer if the mobile network is busy.

When you receive a text message, a notification banner appears at the top of your iPhone screen, as shown, and an alert sound plays. (You can change the text message alert sound in the Settings app's Sound settings; look for the text tone setting.) Tap the notification when it appears to read and to respond to the message.

The notification doesn't hang around forever, however; if you wait for a few seconds, it goes away. That doesn't mean you've lost your chance to read the message. Your Messages app stores the message and even shows you a badge, like the one shown here, to tell you how many unread messages you have waiting to view.

Whether you tap the notification or tap the Messages app icon itself when a badge is visible, you'll see the message, as shown next. You can then do one of the following:

- Type a message in response and tap Send.
- Tap Call to call the number from which the message was sent.
- Tap Add Contact to add the sender to your contacts list.
- Tap FaceTime to engage in a video call with the sender. (We describe FaceTime later in this chapter in the section "Video Chat with FaceTime.")

To get back to your list of text messages so you can send a text to someone else, tap Messages at the top left of the screen.

 SMS text messages don't always come from cell phones. For example, some services provide the capability of sending a text from your computer. In those cases, sending a response or attempting to call the number from which the message was sent may fail.

You can respond to a text message as long as that message remains in the list of text messages on the Messages screen. Tap the message to which you want to respond, type your message in the message field that appears on the next screen, and then tap the Send button.

Send and Receive Texts with iMessage

SMS messages have their virtues—among other things, most mobile phones can send and receive them—but they also have their drawbacks. The biggest drawback is that they cost money; it is not unusual for an active text message user to rack up a significant text messaging bill, as the parents of many teenage children can attest.

However, Apple provides an alternative, cost-free way to send texts: iMessage. This service allows iPhone users to send text messages to other iPhone users, or users of iPads, iPod touches, and Macs running OS X 10.8 Mountain Lion or later.

You don't need to do anything special to send a message with iMessage to another iPhone. When an iPhone is first set up, the phone number is registered with Apple. This allows your iPhone to switch to iMessage automatically when you send a text to another iPhone, bypassing the SMS system. You can tell that you are using iMessage

Now You Know   What Is iMessage?

iMessage is a text messaging service that bypasses the SMS signal path provided by mobile phone carriers and, instead, makes use of Apple's own servers via the Internet. iMessage messages can use either the Internet and data services provided by mobile carriers (3G or 4G) or a Wi-Fi connection to the Internet to transmit and receive messages.

iMessage, unlike SMS, sends and receives messages that are encrypted, which makes them difficult to intercept, and it does not incur a per-message charge from the mobile carrier. Instead, the charge per message is based upon how much data is actually transmitted or received, which is a very small fraction of the charge the same text sent as an SMS message might incur. And if the iMessage is sent over Wi-Fi it's free.

The drawback, of course, is that iMessage can be used to send messages only between Apple devices.

instead of SMS because the Send button is blue, as shown, instead of green, and the New Message screen is titled New iMessage. (Incoming iMessages are also color-coded in blue to help you tell them apart from SMS messages.)

To send a message using iMessage to another iOS device, such as an iPad, or to a Mac running Mountain Lion, the receiving device must first register itself with Apple using an Apple ID and then specify at least one e-mail address or phone number at which messages can be received. Those e-mail addresses or phone numbers are used for addressing purposes only: the messages are still exchanged between the Messages app on your iPhone and the Messages app on the Mac or iOS device. To send a message to an iOS device or a Mac with iMessage from your iPhone, you'll need to address your text message to the e-mail address or phone number that the recipient has registered with Apple.

As with SMS messages, you can respond to any iMessage that is listed on your iPhone's Messages list: tap the message, type your response, and tap Send. Your iPhone figures out whether to send the message as SMS or iMessage; all you have to do is type and tap Send.

Send and Receive Images

From the day that the first mobile phone included a built-in camera, people have wanted to send the pictures it took to others just like they could send text messages. That's why MMS was invented.

   Your iPhone, as any good self-respecting mobile phone should, can send and receive MMS images and videos if the mobile service plan for the iPhone allows it. But more importantly, your iPhone will use iMessage instead of MMS to send images and video any time the receiving device is registered with Apple to use iMessage. When an image or video is sent using iMessage, it can be larger than the 300KB limit to which MMS messages are usually restricted.

Now You Know   What is MMS?

MMS stands for Multimedia Messaging Service and is an expansion to the SMS text messaging service developed by mobile phone service providers. However, unlike SMS, it doesn't limit you to 160 characters like SMS. Instead, the phone converts the image or video into a format that can be transmitted by way of a data connection to the service provider's servers. These servers, in turn, ascertain whether or not the receiving mobile device can handle the image or video media. If the receiving device can accept the media, it downloads the content.

   Typically, providers charge the same amount for an MMS message as they do for an SMS text, but they also charge for the media's data download through the mobile user's data plan. There is no maximum size for MMS media, but generally providers limit each MMS message to 300KB of data.

To send an image, whether via MMS or iMessage, do this:

1. Either create a new message or respond to an existing message, as described earlier in this chapter.

2. Tap the camera button to the left of the text message entry field, as shown:

3. In the dialog that appears (shown next), do one of the following:

- Tap Take Photo Or Video to use your iPhone's camera to take a picture or shoot a short video and send it.

- Tap Choose Existing to send a picture or video from among those stored on your iPhone in the Photos app.

Video Chat with FaceTime

People have been waiting for videophones to become commonplace since the middle of the 20th century. Videophones finally achieved mass-market availability with the iPhone, in the form of FaceTime, Apple's name for the iPhone's video chat feature.

Making use of a small video camera set into the front of your iPhone, FaceTime allows you to make video calls to anyone who uses an iPhone 4 or later or other recent iOS devices that have a front-facing camera, as well as to anyone with a Mac that's running Mac OS X 10.7 Lion or later. (In fact, some Macs running Mac OS X 10.6.6 Snow Leopard may also be able to use it as well, but it became a standard part of the Mac OS in Lion.)

For video calls to another iPhone, you can make a FaceTime call to that iPhone's phone number; for other iOS devices, you use the e-mail address or phone number that device has registered with Apple. (FaceTime uses the e-mail address or phone number simply to identify which device to call; it does not use e-mail or the phone system to make the call itself.)

The FaceTime video chat capability does have some limitations. Because of the amount of data that video consumes—as much as 3MB for each minute—earlier versions of iPhone and iOS required that FaceTime conversations use a Wi-Fi connection to the Internet instead of a mobile carrier's 3G or 4G data connection. With iOS 6, however, that restriction has been removed—that is, as far as Apple is concerned. Whether or not you can actually make a FaceTime call using 3G or 4G depends on the mobile carrier, which may restrict it or require a special data plan.

Interestingly, there is no FaceTime app on the iPhone. Instead, you can initiate a FaceTime call either from an existing voice call or from your Contacts app. (We describe Contacts in Chapter 7.)

To switch a voice call on your iPhone to a FaceTime call, tap the FaceTime icon on the iPhone screen, as shown next, while a voice call is in progress.

To make a FaceTime call from an entry in your Contacts app, do the following:

1. In the Contacts app, select a contact and flick down toward the bottom of the entry, and then tap the FaceTime button:

2. In the list of phone numbers and addresses that appears, tap the one to which you want to make the FaceTime call; a FaceTime-capable number or address usually has a small camera icon next to it, as shown here:

When a FaceTime call is in progress, the video sent from the other device takes up most of your screen, as shown next, with your image appearing in a small box in a corner. You can drag your image box to another corner of the screen if you like. You can also use the controls at the bottom of the screen to mute the call (the icon at left), end the call (center), or switch to or from the higher quality camera on the back of your iPhone (right).

The switch camera feature allows you to continue viewing the person with whom you are speaking, while that person sees video from the iPhone's rear camera—this is handy if you want to show any other people in the room with you (Aunt Sally wants to say, "Hi!"), or scenery (Here's the view from my hotel room), or an interesting object you want that person to see (And this is what happens when you slam the oven door while a soufflé is baking).

Use Social Networks

Telephones are inherently social devices, and telephones with extensive Internet capabilities, like your iPhone, are even more so. In fact, social networking and iPhones seem made for each other; it may not be a complete coincidence that the quickly increasing prominence of social networks in our society has paralleled the explosive growth of the iPhone market. Apple integrated access to one very popular social networking platform, Twitter, in iOS 5, and now iOS 6 adds Facebook integration as well.

Use Twitter

The idea behind Twitter is simple: you create small posts (known as *tweets*) consisting of no more than 140 characters, which other Twitter users can read, share, and reply to with their own tweets. Tweets can contain text, web links, and even links to images that have been uploaded to Twitter's image servers.

Anyone with a Twitter account can read any other Twitter user's tweets (unless that other user has a private Twitter account), but they see your tweets without searching for them only if they *follow* you; similarly, when you use Twitter, you see the tweets of other Twitter users without searching for them only if you follow them. If you like, you can think of tweets as being like SMS messages to the world in general, and to your followers in particular. A Twitter user is identified in Twitter by the user's *handle*, which is the user's account name prefaced by @; for example, Michael's handle is *@lymond*. (Feel free to follow him if you like; bonus points if you know where the name "lymond" comes from.)

Although you don't absolutely *need* the free Twitter app, which you can obtain from the App Store (we cover the App Store in Chapter 11), you'll want to use it for the full Twitter experience. You don't even have to make a special trip to the App Store, though: you can obtain the app from within the Settings app on your iPhone.

We won't explain how to use Twitter itself in this book—there are, in fact, whole books written about Twitter!—but we will explain how to use the Twitter integration built into iOS.

Here's how you set up Twitter integration if you don't yet have the Twitter app:

1. Open the Settings app and flick down to the entry for Twitter; then tap it. You see this screen:

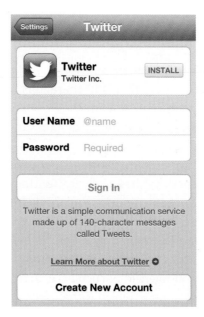

2. Tap the Install button to the right of the Twitter logo to go to the App Store and download it. (Again, see Chapter 11 for more about obtaining apps from the App Store.)

3. After you download the Twitter app, go back into the Settings app and tap Create New Account at the bottom of the screen and fill out the required fields, as shown. Then tap Sign Up at the bottom of the screen.

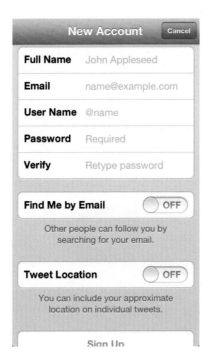

If you already have a Twitter account, follow these steps to set up Twitter integration:

1. Open the Settings app and flick down to the entry for Twitter; then tap it.

2. Tap User Name and enter your Twitter handle, tap Password and enter your Twitter password, and then tap Sign In.

No matter which way you set up Twitter integration, there are two additional, but optional, steps you can take next:

1. On the main Twitter settings screen, tap Update Contacts. This feature searches for the people you follow on Twitter and matches their Twitter handles with the e-mail addresses you have for them in your Contacts app. Then it adds the handles to their contact entries.

2. Flick to the bottom of the Twitter settings screen and enable the apps that you want to access Twitter; the list of apps will vary depending on which Twitter-savvy apps you have installed on your iPhone.

You can have more than one Twitter account listed on your Twitter settings screen. Use the Add Account button on the Twitter settings screen to add them. You can use any of your Twitter accounts with your iPhone's Twitter integration.

Once you have Twitter enabled, using it with apps that allow Twitter integration is simple. In most cases, you can tweet information from an app on your iPhone by tapping a Share icon in the app, which looks like a curved arrow leaping from a box, like this one from the Photos app:

When you tap the Share icon, your iPhone offers a choice of sharing options, such as those shown next. Tap Twitter to tweet the item you want to share on Twitter.

With Twitter integration set up on your iPhone, sharing interesting tidbits from your iPhone apps is usually just a tap or two away.

Use Facebook

If you are among the billion people who already have a Facebook account, I don't need to explain what it is to you; for the rest of you, it's a *social networking service* through which you can exchange messages, images, links, and other information with other people and with organizations. For more details, ask a relative or friend: we'll bet you know a *lot* of people who are on Facebook and who would be happy to tell you more about it!

Setting up Facebook integration on your iPhone is unremarkably similar to the process of setting up Twitter integration:

1. Open the Settings app, flick down to the Facebook entry (it's grouped with the Twitter entry), and tap it to see the Facebook settings screen, shown here:

2. If you don't have the free Facebook app installed on your iPhone, tap the Install button at the top of the settings screen to get it from the App Store (see Chapter 11). You don't absolutely need it to use Facebook integration, but if you are a regular Facebook user you really do want it.

3. If you already have a Facebook account, tap User Name and enter the e-mail address you use with Facebook, tap Password and enter your Facebook password, and then tap Sign In. If you don't have a Facebook account, and have gone to the App Store

to get the app, come back to the Settings app, go back into the Facebook settings (see step 1), tap Create New Account at the bottom of the screen and follow the prompts to sign up for a Facebook account.

4. When you sign in to Facebook on your iPhone for the first time (whether with a new or existing account), Apple provides a detailed list explaining the kinds of access you are granting the Facebook service on your iPhone, as shown next. Read the information and then tap Sign In. (Tap Cancel if you don't want to grant Facebook that access—you can then skip the rest of this section.)

5. Optionally, on the main Facebook settings screen, disable Facebook access to your contacts and calendars by setting the switches to Off, as shown next. This keeps Facebook from adding your Facebook contacts to your Contacts app, from adding your iPhone contacts to your Facebook account, and from posting

items in your Calendar app. (Michael, who regularly uses Facebook, likes to keep his Facebook information separate from the rest of his information and has turned off these access options.)

 The Update All Contacts button does not add the contacts in your Contacts app to your Facebook account like enabling Contacts access does. Instead, it compares the contacts on your iPhone with your Facebook contacts and imports the Facebook user pictures and Facebook user names of matching contacts into your Contacts app. Nothing in your Contacts app is added to your account on Facebook.

With Facebook integration enabled, you can share items much as you can with Twitter, using the Share icon that appears in various apps.

Part III
Sync and Share Data

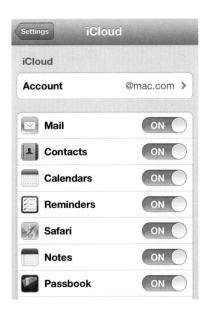

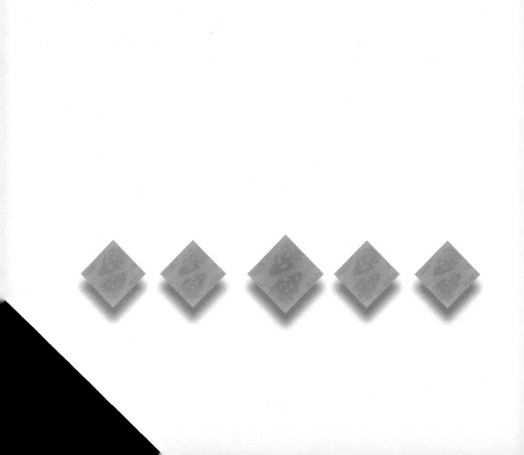

9

Sync Your iPhone
with iTunes

Until the release of iOS 5, syncing an iOS device (be it an iPhone, iPod touch, or iPad) meant backing up and synchronizing your apps, data, and other content with iTunes on a Mac or Windows PC. The release of iOS 5, combined with the introduction of iCloud, made "PC-free" synchronization available, as well as wireless syncing with iTunes. If it is available to you, we recommend using iTunes for a number of reasons, as described in this chapter. Check out Chapter 10 if you want to learn about syncing to iCloud.

 Synchronizing your data means keeping the same information on two or more devices. As an example, when they're "in sync," the contents of your Contacts database on your iPhone matches the contents of the database on your computer (be it Contacts, Address Book, Entourage, or Outlook on a Mac, or Outlook, Outlook Express, Windows Address Book, or Windows Contacts on a Windows PC).

Why Sync to iTunes?

As you will learn in Chapter 10, synchronizing to iCloud places storage limitations on the amount of content you can sync. Although your iTunes Store purchases, iTunes Match content (if you paid for this service), and Photo Stream don't count against the 5GB of free space, everything else does, including any videos you have that didn't come from the iTunes Store, ebooks that you didn't buy from the iBookstore, and all other data (e-mail, Pages, Numbers, Keynote documents, and so on). Video, in particular, will chomp through 5GB faster than a horde of locusts through a grain field.

Additionally, syncing with iTunes is much faster than syncing to iCloud, even if you do so wirelessly. Most service providers put a throughput limit on uploads that makes uploads much slower than downloads, which are also slower than a Wi-Fi connection on your local network. If you use the cable that came with your iPhone to connect to your Mac or PC, you'll sync even faster.

iTunes from On High

iTunes is a large application that has grown from the basic SoundJam "jukebox" application Apple acquired from Casady & Greene at the turn of the century and relaunched as Apple's iTunes. In addition to ripping CDs, playing audio, organizing audio into playlists, and syncing that audio content to the MP3 players of yore, iTunes now manages syncing with a plethora of devices, including the old-style MP3 players, the vast panoply of iPod models introduced in the past decade-plus, iOS devices, and Apple TVs. In addition to the music that was its raison d'être, iTunes now manages iOS apps, audiobooks, ebooks, videos, ringtones, browser bookmarks, contacts, calendars, and other data.

The iTunes window is shown in Figure 9-1, with an iPhone and an iPad connected, and the iPhone named TheLeash selected in the Source List (that's the pane on the left, sometimes called a *sidebar*).

Figure 9-1   *The Summary tab of the iTunes window*

When an iOS device is selected in the Source List, the large pane, called the *content pane*, displays a series of tabs across the top:

- **Summary**   This title is, in our opinion, a partial misnomer, because it doesn't summarize the other settings, but it does give a summary of your iPhone serial number and other information and offers a collection of backup and syncing options.

- **Info**   This is where you specify what information, such as contacts, calendars, and notes, gets synced.

- **Apps**   Visit this pane to specify which apps go on your iPhone, to choose where the apps appear on your Home screen, and to transfer files between your computer and the apps that use them.

- **Tones**   This sparsely populated pane controls which tones you want to sync with your iPhone for use as ringtones and text tones. If you haven't added any ringtones to your iPhone or your iTunes library, you won't see this tab on your screen.

- **Music**   Probably one of the most frequently visited panes, Music is where you determine which music is synced between your computer and your iPhone.

- **Movies**   Specify video content that has its Media Kind set as Movie to sync here.

- **TV Shows**   Specify video content that has its Media Kind set as TV Show to sync here.

- **Podcasts**   Specify which podcasts and podcast episodes to sync in this tab.

- **iTunes U**   Manage iTunes U courses to sync under this tab.

- **Books**   Manage electronic book (iBooks) and audiobook syncing in this pane.

- **Photos**   Photos are a one-way sync, going only from your computer to your iPhone. Under this tab, you specify whether you're syncing photos from a folder structure (Mac or Windows) or from an application's database: iPhoto or Aperture on a Mac or Photoshop Elements 8 or later under Windows.

At the bottom of the content pane is a bar that indicates how much content of each type is present on your iPhone, in one of three displays as shown next. You switch between displays by clicking a size, quantity, or time at the bottom of the display. The difference in the three displays is subtle: the first illustration shows the space consumed, the second shows the quantity in each category, and the third shows the duration (for audio/video) and space otherwise.

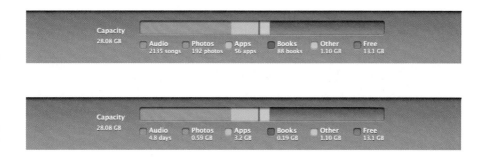

The Summary Tab

The Summary tab (Figure 9-1) includes four sections: iPhone, Version, Backup, and Options.

iPhone Section

When you set up your iPhone, you had the option of naming it. (Dennis chose TheLeash because his wife talked him into getting a cell phone so she could call him when he was walking the dogs or running errands.) Capacity shows how many gigabytes of storage are available. (Available capacity is always less than the nominal storage.)

The next three statistics are simply the initial information. If you click the information, the statistics displayed change, as follows:

- **Software Version**   When clicked, displays the Build Number, the internal sequencing number Apple uses to designate which version of the source code was used to create the software on this iPhone.

- **Serial Number**   When clicked, toggles to display the Unique Device ID (UDID), a 30-byte-long (60 hexadecimal digits) string used to identify your iPhone uniquely (hence the name) for determining whether your phone can install apps that haven't come from the App Store and, if so, which ones. iPhone developers need to register the UDIDs of the iPhones on which they intend to install software under development for testing purposes.

- **Phone Number**   A trifecta. First, the obvious number is your telephone number. Click once and you see the IMEI (International Mobile Equipment Identity) number. Click again for the ICCID, the serial number of your iPhone's SIM card.

Version Section

Version is a small, self-explanatory section with two buttons: Check for Updates (which toggles to Update when an update is available) and Restore. Both offer a description and explanation to their right.

When updates to your iPhone software are available, we recommend installing them, as they invariably fix bugs, add features, or improve performance (or some combination of the preceding).

Restore performs a factory reset on your iPhone (except that it installs the latest iOS release, rather than the one that might have been on the phone from the factory), and it's used mostly for troubleshooting purposes or to return your phone to a pristine state before you sell it, trade it in, or pass it on to a family member. Note that this restore is not the same as restoring your phone from a previous backup.

Backup Section

This is another self-explanatory section. Select the radio button appropriate to whether you want the backups on iCloud or on this computer. If you opt for the computer, you can also select a checkbox indicating that the backup should be encrypted. When you back up to your computer via iTunes, you don't have the same 5GB storage limit that you have with iCloud. These backups let you restore your phone (or load all your old data onto a new phone) to the last saved state.

Finally, if you back up to the computer, the date and time of the last such backup is displayed.

Options Section

Think of this section as the preferences area. This is where you turn on wireless syncing, toggle whether iTunes launches automatically when the iPhone is plugged into the computer, determine whether a sync will try to copy all your songs and videos or just those you specify under the corresponding tabs, whether high-definition video should be downsized to standard-definition video to save space, whether audio should be downsampled to 128, 192, or 256 Kbps Advanced Audio Coding (AAC), and whether you want to manage music and video manually by dragging individual entries in those categories onto (or off of) your iPhone within iTunes.

Info Tab

Under the Info tab, you'll find sections for Contacts, Calendars, Mail Accounts, Other, and Advanced to sync. Here you'll find information rather than media.

Sync Contacts

If you select to sync your contacts between the iPhone and the computer, you can sync from your Contacts (OS X 10.8) or Address Book (Mac OS X 10.7 and earlier) applications on a Mac or Outlook on Windows. Additionally, as shown in the following illustration, if you have Yahoo! or Google contact lists, you can sync those. You can also specify that contacts created on the iPhone that aren't in groups should be added to a specified group on your computer.

☐ **Sync Contacts**

⦿ All contacts
○ Selected groups

☐ Add contacts created outside of groups on this iPhone to: [⬍]
☐ Sync Yahoo! Address Book contacts [Configure…]
☐ Sync Google Contacts [Configure…]

Your contacts are being synced with iCloud over the air. You can also choose to sync contacts with this computer. This may result in duplicated data showing on your device.

Syncing contacts with both iCloud and the computer can (and probably will) result in duplicated contacts on your iPhone.

Sync Calendars

Like Contacts, syncing calendars between the iPhone and the computer works with the OS X–supplied applications and the iPhone, in this case Calendar or iCal on a Mac, or between Outlook and the iPhone on Windows. Similarly, as shown next, you can specify to sync all or specific calendars within those applications. In addition, you can sync Google calendars. You will find Reminders in the list of possible calendars to sync, and your Reminders will sync if you select All Calendars.

Syncing calendars with both iCloud and the computer can (and probably will) result in duplicated events on your iPhone.

Sync Mail Accounts

You can sync any or all mail accounts from the computer to the iPhone (but not the other way around), as shown next. Additionally, only the account information is synced, not the actual contents of any mailbox on your computer, which makes sense, because you almost certainly don't want gigabytes of archived e-mails clogging up your phone's storage.

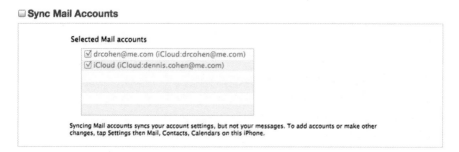

Other

This is a catch-all for other data types to sync and could grow if Apple provides more apps of the sort. At the moment, you can sync bookmarks between Safari on your iPhone and Safari on either Mac or Windows or Internet Explorer on Windows, and you can sync Notes to another compatible program (such as Outlook) if you use them, as shown:

Advanced

Every once in a while, you might mess up the data in one of the previously described categories (usually as a result of inadvertently deleting something or by syncing both to iCloud and the computer). The Advanced section gives you the chance to do a one-time replacement of the data in one or more categories with the data on the computer, giving you a fresh start, as shown next:

Advanced

Replace information on this iPhone
- ☐ Contacts
- ☐ Calendars
- ☐ Mail Accounts
- ☐ Notes

During the next sync only, iTunes will replace the selected information on this iPhone with information from this computer.

Apps Tab

The Apps tab, shown in Figure 9-2, is one of our favorite tabs, mostly because of its Home screen management functionality that we find faster and easier to use than going through the jiggling icon dance on our iPhones, especially when we want to move app icons to a different Home screen.

If you opt to sync apps (select the Sync Apps checkbox), you can click the pop-up menu to see your apps grouped by name, kind, category, date, or size.

Select the checkboxes for the apps you want on your iPhone and deselect those you don't want to be synced to your phone. Alternatively, you can drag an app's entry in the list to the Home screen (or the thumbnail of a Home screen) displayed on the right, placing it exactly where you want it, even inside a folder. We find this a lot easier than moving it on the iPhone after the App Store places it where it wants.

In the Home screen display, you can click a Home screen thumbnail in the list on the right to make it the active Home screen, drag an icon from the active Home screen to the thumbnail where you want it moved, and do all the obvious management chores such as creating folders in one easily managed location. We think you'll really like this feature if you have a lot of apps or frequently rearrange the collection you have.

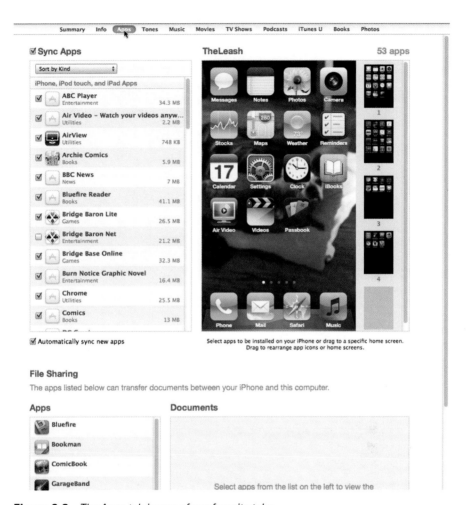

Figure 9-2 *The Apps tab is one of our favorite tabs.*

 And here's one more thing you can do with iTunes Home screen management: You can drag the thumbnails in the list on the far right up and down, changing the order of your Home screen. Try that on your iPhone!

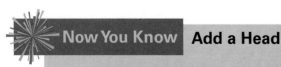

Now You Know **Add a Head**

With regard to apps, if you're curious as to what "kind" means, here's the scoop. There are three kinds of apps for iOS:

- Apps written for the iPhone and iPod touch can run on any iOS device, but run on the iPad at iPhone screen resolution only, rather than the full resolution of the iPad's display.

- A Universal app runs on the iPhone, iPod touch, and iPad at the full resolution of the device's screen.

- An iPad app cannot be run on your iPhone, so it will be disabled (grayed out) in the list of apps.

Tones Tab

This is where you specify whether to sync all acquired tones or specific acquired tones to your iPhone. When you select Selected Tones, a list of the tones in your iTunes Ringtones collection appears, letting you pick and choose.

Now You Know **Add More Tones**

You can purchase ringtones in the iTunes Store (the ones we've perused cost $1.29 each at the time we're writing this). You can also purchase ringtones or obtain free ringtones at various sites on the Web ("iPhone ringtones" is a good search term to find such sites), but you should be cautious about giving out personal information on these sites. Do a little investigation to make sure they're not going to distribute your information to all and sundry. Most are legitimate, but scammers and spammers are always popping up on the Web.

Alternatively, there are utilities available to help you create your own ringtones on your computer. iRinger (www.iringer.net) and Ringtone Expressions (www.gx-5.com) are two well-regarded Windows utilities for this purpose, and we like Ambrosia Softworks iToner (www.AmbrosiaSW.com) for the Mac.

Finally, if you're a Mac user, your Mac came with GarageBand. One of GarageBand's less publicized capabilities is that it can be used to create ringtones. You can start with audio from your iTunes Library, create your ringtone using GarageBand's loops and instruments, or record your own ringtone using your Mac and a microphone. We create a lot of ringtones out of recordings, such as, "This is Michael calling, please pick up." GarageBand is free and easy, and it's a nice fringe benefit of being a Mac-owning iPhone user.

Music Tab

We don't know of any iPhone users who don't have some music on their phones. In fact, we don't know of any iPhone users with a Mac or Windows PC who don't already use iTunes to maintain a library of music. So if you are syncing with iTunes, it is a virtual given that you will be putting all or part of your iTunes library on your iPhone. In any event, the Music tab is where you specify what, if anything, in the Music category of your iTunes library gets synced.

At the top of the Music tab, select the Sync Music checkbox if you want any of your music synced. If you don't want to sync your music, for whatever reason, or if you manually want to micro-manage which music goes on your iPhone (see the "Summary Tab" section earlier in this chapter), leave Sync Music unchecked and skip to the "Movies Tab" section.

Still with us? In the top section of the Music tab, select either to sync your entire music library or selected playlists, artists, albums, and genres. If you opt for the latter, you'll see the four lists shown in Figure 9-3, but with your content rather than Dennis's content.

iTunes includes music videos in the Music library alongside music. If you want music videos to sync, select that checkbox. If you want

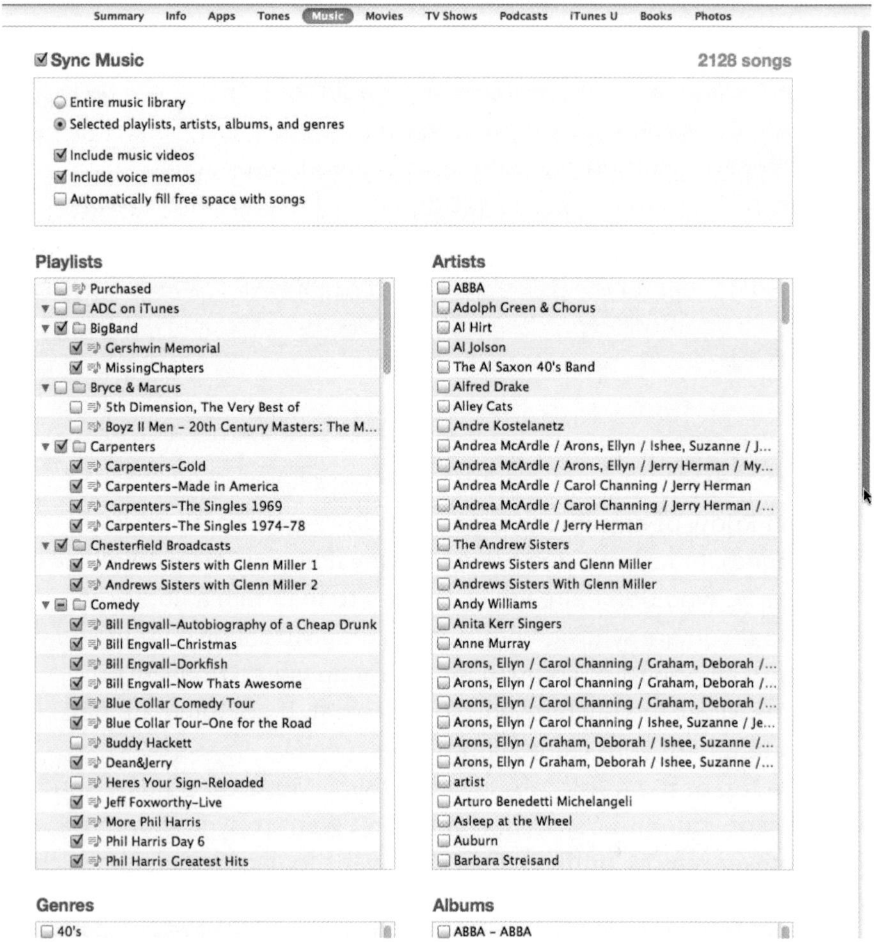

Figure 9-3 *The Music tab*

recorded voice memos from your iPhone or iPod touch to sync, select the obvious checkbox. The final checkbox in this group, Automatically Fill Free Space With Songs, tells iTunes to fill any free space on your iPhone with songs.

 Obviously, if you're syncing your entire library and there's still free space, iTunes won't find any unsynced songs to use to fill the space. Further, filling free space with songs isn't going to leave you any room for storing photos or movies, creating documents, adding apps, or utilizing any of the other cool features your iPhone offers—so we recommend against this "feature."

The four lists that appear when you opt for syncing selected playlists, artists, albums, and genres display what's in your library. Pick and choose what you want synced from any or all of the lists by selecting the corresponding checkboxes. Don't worry; if a song appears in more than one playlist and is also included in the songs for a selected artist, album, and genre, only one copy is placed on your iPhone.

Movies Tab

Your iPhone is a fine personal video viewer, with its high-resolution screen. If you have movies in your iTunes library that you want synced to your iPhone, you make that happen in the Movies tab by selecting the Sync Movies checkbox, as shown in Figure 9-4.

If you select the Automatically Include checkbox in the Sync Movies section, you can choose, from the pop-up menu shown next, to have all movies or some of the most recent or the most recent unwatched movies synced. If you don't select the Automatically Include checkbox, you will see the two lists shown in Figure 9-4, where you can pick and choose the individual movies to sync.

√ all
1 most recent
3 most recent
5 most recent
10 most recent

all unwatched
1 most recent unwatched
3 most recent unwatched
5 most recent unwatched
10 most recent unwatched
1 least recent unwatched
3 least recent unwatched
5 least recent unwatched
10 least recent unwatched

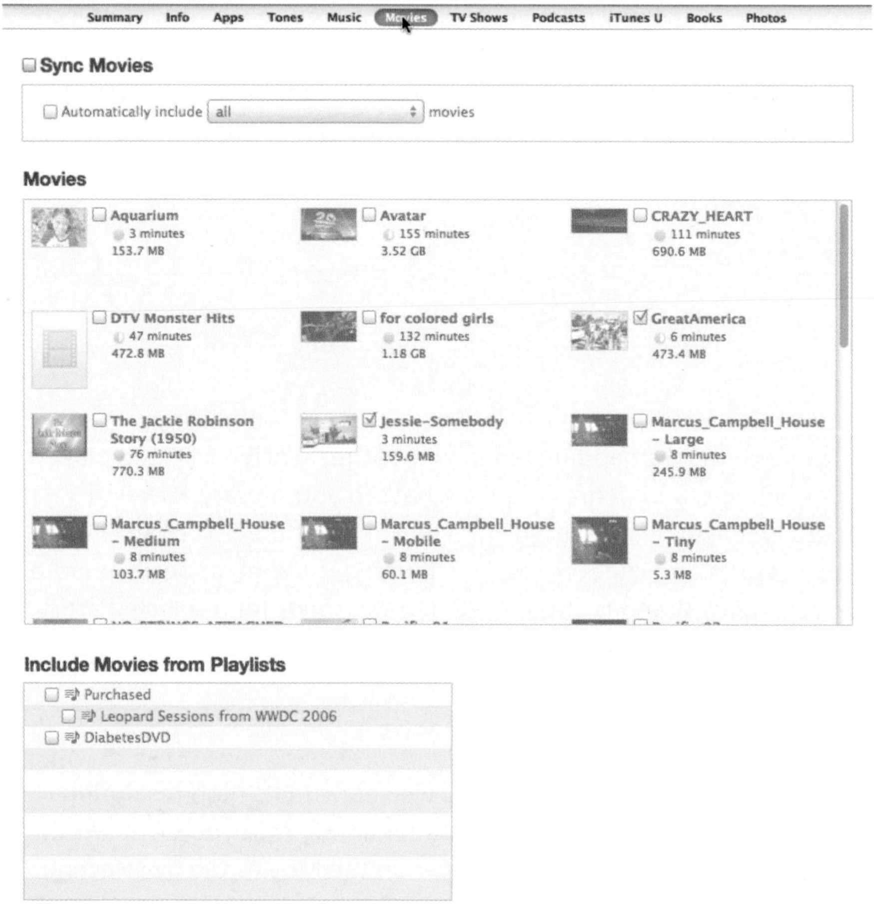

| Summary | Info | Apps | Tones | Music | **Movies** | TV Shows | Podcasts | iTunes U | Books | Photos |

☐ **Sync Movies**

☐ Automatically include [all   ⇕] movies

Movies

☐ Aquarium ○ 3 minutes 153.7 MB	☐ Avatar ○ 155 minutes 3.52 GB	☐ CRAZY_HEART ○ 111 minutes 690.6 MB
☐ DTV Monster Hits ○ 47 minutes 472.8 MB	☐ for colored girls ○ 132 minutes 1.18 GB	☑ GreatAmerica ○ 6 minutes 473.4 MB
☐ The Jackie Robinson Story (1950) ○ 76 minutes 770.3 MB	☑ Jessie–Somebody 3 minutes 159.6 MB	☐ Marcus_Campbell_House – Large ○ 8 minutes 245.9 MB
☐ Marcus_Campbell_House – Medium ○ 8 minutes 103.7 MB	☐ Marcus_Campbell_House – Mobile ○ 8 minutes 60.1 MB	☐ Marcus_Campbell_House – Tiny ○ 8 minutes 5.3 MB

Include Movies from Playlists

☐ 🎞 Purchased
   ☐ 🎞 Leopard Sessions from WWDC 2006
☐ 🎞 DiabetesDVD

Figure 9-4   *The Movies tab*

TV Shows Tab

TV Shows in your iTunes library are also candidates for syncing. Select the Sync TV Shows checkbox if you want some or all of your collected TV shows synced to the iPhone, as shown in Figure 9-5.

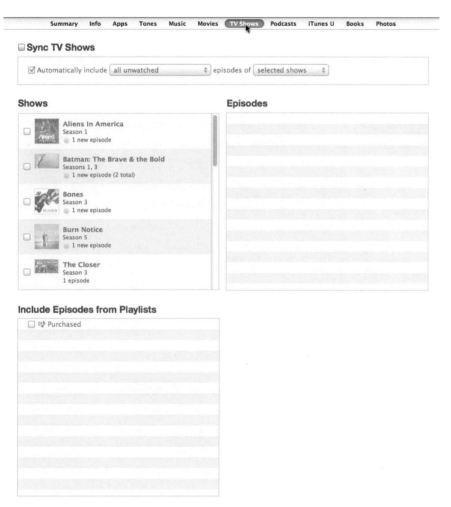

Figure 9-5   *The TV Shows tab*

The two pop-up menus to the right of the Automatically Include checkbox, as shown here, let you specify whether all episodes or only unwatched episodes should be synced and whether that applies to all shows or only selected shows (use the list boxes to pick and choose).

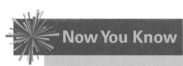

Now You Know **Classify Your Video Files**

Unless you acquired the video from the iTunes Store or used
hardware and software such as Elgato's (www.elgato.com)
wonderful EyeTV packages that tell iTunes that a TV show is a TV
show, iTunes treats all video, initially, as movies. You can use the Info
pane in iTunes' Get Info dialog to change the media type, but until
you do so, some TV shows and music videos as well as podcasts
acquired from web sites will be miscategorized.

Podcasts Tab

Podcasts are handled identically to TV shows, as you can see in Figure 9-6.
   Check out the TV Shows tab coverage and you will know how to
work with podcasts and their episodes.

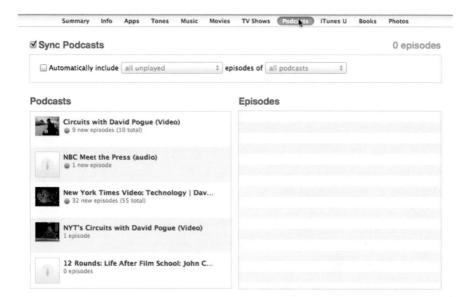

Figure 9-6   *The Podcasts tab*

iTunes U Tab

In our opinions, iTunes U, shown in Figure 9-7, is one of the very best things Apple has done for its customers. In partnership with hundreds of (K–12) schools, colleges, and universities around the world, top-quality courses, classes, and seminars are available to you, and almost everything is free of charge.

If you've seen how TV shows and podcasts are managed, you already know how to manage iTunes U courses. If not, check out the "TV Shows Tab" section earlier in the chapter.

 As shown in Figures 9-6 and 9-7, a small circle appears to the left of a podcast or lecture's name, and the same holds true for TV show episodes. An empty circle means that the item hasn't yet been viewed; a full circle means that you have watched it; and a partially-filled circle indicates how much of an episode has been watched.

| Summary | Info | Apps | Tones | Music | Movies | TV Shows | Podcasts | iTunes U | Books | Photos |

☐ **Sync iTunes U**

☑ Automatically include [all unplayed ⇕] items of [all collections ⇕]

Collections

MIT OCW: 18.03 Differential Equations, S...
● 8 new episodes (10 total)

Items

Figure 9-7   *The iTunes U tab*

Books Tab

We write books (obviously) and we edit books, but most of all, we read books. Neither of us listens to audiobooks, but we have friends and family members who are very fond of what started out as "books on tape," became "books on disc," and now is just called "audiobooks" that are listened to on iPods and similar devices around the world.

Following the consistent interface seen thus far, as shown in Figure 9-8, you select the Sync Books checkbox if you want to sync ebooks (short for electronic books) to your iPhone.

Select All Books or Selected Books in the top section. This section is not marked as applying to all ebooks, but that's actually the case.

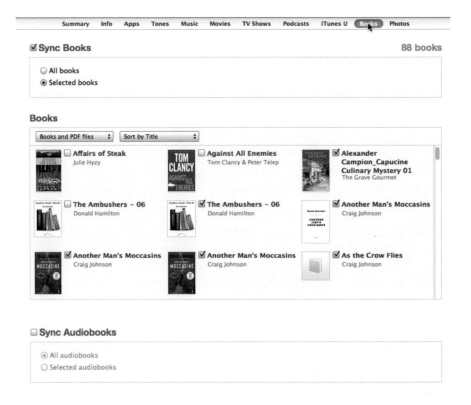

Figure 9-8 *The Books tab*

The Sync Audiobooks section has its own pair of radio buttons near the bottom of the Books tab.

In the Books section, if you opted for Selected Books, you'll see checkboxes next to book titles (and usually an image of the jacket cover). The items displayed for syncing can be filtered using the first pop-up menu to Books And PDF Files, Only Books, or Only PDF Files, and the display order can be sorted by title, by author, or by date, which is controlled by the second pop-up. Select the checkboxes next to the titles you want to sync.

If you have audiobooks to sync, select the Sync Audiobooks checkbox and repeat the drill just described to sync all or selected audiobooks; only sorting is available at this point, because there is only one type of audiobook.

Photos Tab

The Photos tab, shown in Figure 9-9, is dedicated to managing which photos on your computer are synced to your iPhone. This sync is one-way. iTunes manages moving photos from your computer to the iPhone, but if you want photos on your iPhone brought onto your computer, whatever application you have set up to retrieve photos from a camera or memory card handles that movement.

If selected, the Sync Photos From checkbox offers a pop-up menu, as shown next, where you can designate the source of the photos to move to the iPhone. On the Mac, the choice is usually between iPhoto or a folder, as shown next, where you designate the folder structure, such as your Photos folder. If you have Aperture installed, that option will also appear in the pop-up menu. On a Windows computer, your choice will be a folder or, if you have it installed, Photoshop Elements (version 8 or later).

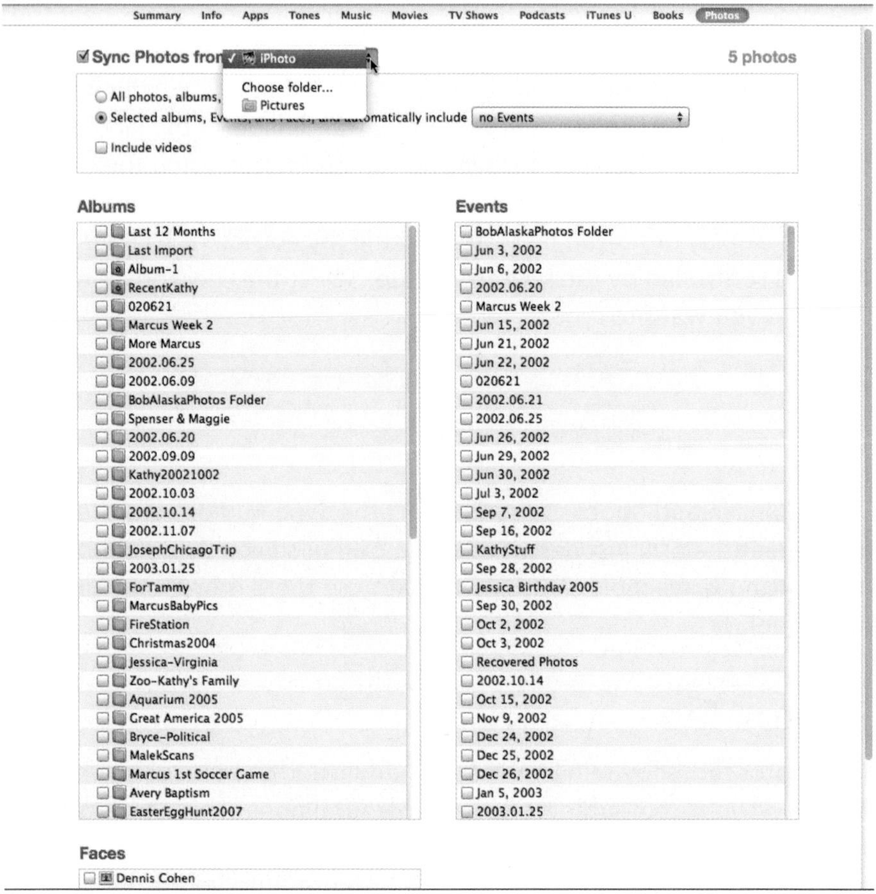

| Summary | Info | Apps | Tones | Music | Movies | TV Shows | Podcasts | iTunes U | Books | Photos |

☑ Sync Photos from ✓ 📷 iPhoto   5 photos

  Choose folder...
  📁 Pictures

○ All photos, albums,
● Selected albums, Ev.... ...omatically include no Events ⬍

☐ Include videos

Albums

☐ Last 12 Months	
☐ Last Import	
☐ Album-1	
☐ RecentKathy	
☐ 020621	
☐ Marcus Week 2	
☐ More Marcus	
☐ 2002.06.25	
☐ 2002.06.09	
☐ BobAlaskaPhotos Folder	
☐ Spenser & Maggie	
☐ 2002.06.20	
☐ 2002.09.09	
☐ Kathy20021002	
☐ 2002.10.03	
☐ 2002.10.14	
☐ 2002.11.07	
☐ JosephChicagoTrip	
☐ 2003.01.25	
☐ ForTammy	
☐ MarcusBabyPics	
☐ FireStation	
☐ Christmas2004	
☐ Jessica-Virginia	
☐ Zoo-Kathy's Family	
☐ Aquarium 2005	
☐ Great America 2005	
☐ Bryce-Political	
☐ MalekScans	
☐ Marcus 1st Soccer Game	
☐ Avery Baptism	
☐ EasterEggHunt2007	

Events

☐ BobAlaskaPhotos Folder
☐ Jun 3, 2002
☐ Jun 6, 2002
☐ 2002.06.20
☐ Marcus Week 2
☐ Jun 15, 2002
☐ Jun 21, 2002
☐ Jun 22, 2002
☐ 020621
☐ 2002.06.21
☐ 2002.06.25
☐ Jun 26, 2002
☐ Jun 29, 2002
☐ Jun 30, 2002
☐ Jul 3, 2002
☐ Sep 7, 2002
☐ Sep 16, 2002
☐ KathyStuff
☐ Sep 28, 2002
☐ Jessica Birthday 2005
☐ Sep 30, 2002
☐ Oct 2, 2002
☐ Oct 3, 2002
☐ Recovered Photos
☐ 2002.10.14
☐ Oct 15, 2002
☐ Nov 9, 2002
☐ Dec 24, 2002
☐ Dec 25, 2002
☐ Dec 26, 2002
☐ Jan 5, 2003
☐ 2003.01.25

Faces

☐ Dennis Cohen

Figure 9-9   *The Photos tab*

In the top section of the Photos tab, you can specify All Photos, Events, Albums, and Faces or Selected Albums Photos, Events, and Faces. (Faces result from tagging using facial recognition features built into iPhoto and Aperture. The facial recognition feature in Photoshop Elements is not recognized.) If you opt for the Selected option, you see lists of Albums, Events, and Faces. Do what should be natural by now and select the checkboxes for the items you want to sync.

10

Use iCloud and Other Cloud Services

When it comes to digital devices such as your iPhone, the *cloud* is, pardon the pun, a nebulous concept. The term itself comes from the template symbol used by data processing professionals when they draw charts of where and how data flows through a system: the cloud symbol represents a source or destination of data that is beyond the particular system components being described, such as somewhere else on a local network or on the Internet.

For the user of digital devices like you, the cloud is usually somewhere on the Internet, and *cloud services* are those services, offered by companies like Apple, that give you the capability of stashing, retrieving, and updating your information on their servers and networks. You don't need to know—and, in fact, cannot easily find out—exactly where and how your data is stored and managed on these external networks and servers. It is the job of a cloud service to handle all the pesky details of how your information is kept and retrieved: all that matters to you is that you can get your stuff when you need it, whether the information is a simple shopping list or the last 1000 photos you took with your iPhone camera.

In this chapter we look at the collection of cloud-based data services that Apple calls iCloud, and we glance at a couple of other cloud services and explain how you can take advantage of them with your iPhone.

Sync and Back Up with iCloud

Exactly what iCloud is and does is as difficult to describe as a cloud itself: its shape cannot be seen completely from where you stand and the shape that it has changes as Apple continues to refine it. You can think of iCloud as the way you access, share, store, and back up your "stuff," from documents, to photos, to music, and much more.

Many of the built-in apps on your iPhone (see Chapter 5) can synchronize their information with other iOS devices or with a Mac or PC. We've already described in Chapter 7 how your Contacts and Calendar apps can share their information with other devices, but they're not the only apps that can do that. For example, if you have an iPhone and an iPad, both of them can have the same notes in their respective Notes apps by using iCloud to synchronize the notes: make a new note on your iPhone and it appears within seconds on your iPad, or change a note on your iPad and that change appears almost immediately on your iPhone (that is, of course, if both devices have an Internet connection).

iCloud also offers the capability of backing up the information stored in the apps on your devices. For example, suppose (heaven forfend) that you lose your iPhone and have to get a new one. You can use your iPhone backup stored with iCloud to restore the data you had on your lost iPhone to your new iPhone, so that the loss of your phone won't be compounded by the loss of the information you had on it.

Some of the apps you obtain from the App Store (see Chapter 11) may be iCloud-enabled as well. For example, the Pages word processing app for the iPhone can store its documents in iCloud; you can then edit those documents with the Pages application on the Mac, and vice versa. Books that you read in the iBooks app (see Chapter 13) on your iPhone automatically sync your notes, bookmarks, and the current page with iBooks on another iOS device that uses the same iCloud account, so you can start reading a book on your iPhone and later pick up where you left off on your iPad.

When you obtain apps from the App Store, you can have iCloud set up to download those apps automatically to any other iOS devices you may have. This also holds true for music, movies, and TV shows you buy from the iTunes Store and for books you buy from the iBookstore. In addition, an optional iCloud service you can purchase, called iTunes Match (see "What's Free and What Costs on iCloud" later in this chapter), lets you store your entire iTunes library (or at least the first 25,000 songs from your library) in Apple's cloud—you don't need to take up space on your iPhone with all your music, because you can access the songs you want to hear from the cloud at any time.

Photos can also be synced among your devices with the Photo Stream component of iCloud: as many as 1000 of your most recently taken photos can be sent to iCloud automatically and shared with your other iOS devices, as well as with the iPhoto or Aperture library on your Mac or with the Pictures Library on your PC. You can use iCloud to create photo streams to share with other iCloud users and with the world at large, too, as we explain in Chapter 14.

You can expect that Apple will add more features and capability to iCloud over time, so if you are at all interested in being able to share your iPhone's data with any other iOS devices you own and your computer, it's worth checking out iCloud.

Set Up iCloud on Your iPhone

In Chapter 1 we showed how signing up for an iCloud account is an iPhone setup option, and we encouraged you to take advantage of it then. However, if you didn't follow our advice, no worries, because you can do it now:

1. Open the Settings app and tap iCloud.

2. On the iCloud settings screen, sign in to an existing iCloud account (if you already have one) or create a new account.

If you already have an iCloud account and are signed into it on your iPhone, the iCloud settings screen looks something like this:

Below the Account button on the iCloud settings screen are a series of switches you can use to enable iCloud's services:

- **Mail**   Tap this on to have mail addressed to your iCloud e-mail account arrive on your iPhone.

- **Contacts**, **Calendars**, **Reminders**, **Notes**, and **Passbook**   These switches control whether the information in these apps are synchronized with iCloud's servers, so that any changes you make in them appear on any other devices that synchronize the same type of data with iCloud. For example, a PC can synchronize its Outlook contacts list and its calendars with iCloud, and the Outlook data appears on your phone in the Contacts and Calendars apps, and vice versa. Similarly, the Contacts, Calendars, Reminders, and Notes applications on a Mac running OS X Mountain Lion and those on your iPhone can remain in sync whenever you make a change on your Mac or on your iPhone. (Some, but not all, of these apps can sync on earlier versions of Mac OS X.) And, of course, all of these apps remain in sync with the same apps on any other iOS devices you have that use the same iCloud account.

- **Safari**   Tapping this on keeps the bookmarks and reading lists in Safari on your iPhone synchronized with Safari on your Mac and other iOS devices, or with Explorer on a PC running Windows Vista or later.

Farther down the main iCloud settings screen are additional options, shown here:

- **Photo Stream**   Tap this to turn your own Photo Stream on or off and to turn on or off the capability of creating Shared Photo Streams. Photo Stream is discussed in more detail in Chapter 14.

- **Documents & Data**   Tap this to see a screen on which you can enable or disable whether apps other than those listed on the main iCloud settings screen can store their documents and their data in iCloud for use with other iOS devices or computers (such as, for example, Apple's Pages word processing app). You can also choose whether or not to use a cellular connection to transfer data and documents to iCloud when a Wi-Fi connection is not available.

- **Find My iPhone**   When this is turned on, your iPhone can be located by its cellular or Wi-Fi connection whether it is awake or asleep. (Note that you must have Location Services enabled for this feature to work.) If you misplace your iPhone, you can log into iCloud on any computer at www.icloud.com and see where your iPhone is on a map. You can also have your iPhone produce a distinctive sound (useful for finding it when your iPhone has slipped beneath the sofa cushions), display a message (helpful if you think a friend might have scooped it up), and lock or even erase it's contents if you think your iPhone has fallen into a thief's hands.

Tapping the Storage & Backup button on the main iCloud settings screen takes you to the Storage & Backup screen, where you can see how much of your online iCloud storage you have used, as shown next:

When you create an iCloud account, you automatically have 5GB of free storage, which is enough for many casual iCloud users. If, however, you plan to make extensive use of iCloud for storing documents from your apps, you can tap Change Storage Plan to buy an additional 10GB, 20GB, or 50GB of storage from Apple at a cost of $20, $40, or $100, respectively, per year. You can also turn on the iCloud Backup option to back up your iPhone's data to iCloud whenever you plug it in and have a Wi-Fi connection. You can tap the Back Up Now button at the bottom of the screen to back up your iPhone to iCloud immediately. Note that if you do not want to back up automatically with iCloud, we encourage you to back up using iTunes so that you have up-to-date copies of your phone's data.

To help you decide whether you may need additional iCloud storage, and to see and control which apps are using iCloud storage and how much storage each is using, tap the Manage Storage button on the Storage & Backup screen. This displays the Manage Storage screen, shown here:

The Documents & Data section on the Manage Storage screen shows you how much iCloud storage various apps on your iPhone are using; tap the name of an app to see a detailed account of how the app is using its iCloud storage. The Backups section at the top of the Manage Storage screen shows each device that is using the iCloud account for backups and how much storage each of them is using. Tap the name of a device to see an Info screen:

In addition to showing you the size of the latest backup, the Info screen shows you how large the next one will be and how much storage is being used by each app's backup. The Info screen is about more than just information, however. You can use it to control which apps back up and which don't—just tap to turn off the switch by each app you don't want backed up to iCloud.

You may want to turn off backups for any apps that may have their contents backed up by other means. For example, the Camera Roll on Michael's iPhone, shown in the preceding illustration, requires 1.9GB of backup space, but because he has copied the pictures about which he cares to his iPhoto library on his Mac (which he backs up with other methods), he could easily turn off his Camera Roll backup without having to worry about losing any important pictures should something happen to his iPhone (besides, his most recent pictures are already stored in iCloud for free via his Photo Stream).

You can use other iCloud services but still back up your iPhone to your iTunes library on your computer, as we described in Chapter 9, instead of backing up to iCloud. This can be faster, and, more importantly, it makes your iCloud storage allocation available for other purposes. If you want to stay within the free 5GB allotment you get with iCloud and not purchase additional storage, backing up to iTunes can help you achieve that.

In addition to checking out the settings located behind the iCloud button in the Settings app, you should take a quick trip to the iTunes & App Stores settings for a few additional iCloud-related settings. Tap iTunes & App Stores from the main Settings app screen to see the iTunes & App Stores settings, shown here:

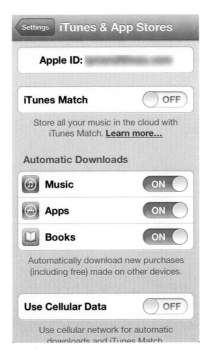

The three settings in the Automatic Downloads section control whether iCloud automatically downloads to your iPhone any purchases that you make in Apple's iTunes Music Store (see Chapter 12), its App

Store (see Chapter 11), and its iBookstore (see Chapter 13). You can also choose whether or not to restrict such downloads only to those times when you have a Wi-Fi connection, to help reduce data charges on your mobile service plan. If you have more than one iOS device, automatic downloads ensure that all of your devices have the same apps and purchased media.

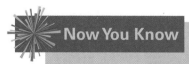

What's Free and What Costs on iCloud

iCloud is an umbrella name that covers, as you've seen, a variety of services and capabilities: mail, syncing, document storage, picture storage, backups, and more. When it comes to the storage services that iCloud provides, some are free, some are only free within limits, and some cost money right from the start. Here's a breakdown of what costs what:

- **Purchases**   After you purchase something from any of Apple's online stores, you do not have to pay a second time to download it to other iOS devices. Therefore, you can delete items you purchase from your iPhone and download them again later as often as you like—in essence treating the online stores as a free backup location for your purchased apps, books, music, movies, and TV shows. Note that backups to iCloud do not include the apps or media, since you can download them again at any time or, if you sync with iTunes, you can restore them from the copies in your iTunes library.

- **Pictures**   Pictures in your personal Photo Stream are stored and downloaded free. The Photo Stream contains only the last 1000 pictures you have taken, though, so you may want to back up older pictures some other way. You are charged for the storage required to back up the pictures in your Camera Roll, however. (See Chapter 14 for more about Photo Stream and the Camera Roll.)

- **Contacts, Calendars, Safari, Notes, Reminders, and Passbook** You are not charged for the storage used to support syncing these items with iCloud.
- **Find My iPhone** This service is free.
- **Mail** The storage used for your iCloud mail is counted against your iCloud storage allocation.
- **Data & Documents** Storage used by apps for documents and data is counted against your iCloud storage allocation.
- **Backups** These are counted against your iCloud storage allocation.
- **iTunes Match** This service does not count against your iCloud allocation, but it does require a separate yearly fee for storage of up to 25,000 songs; the fee is currently $25 per year.

Set Up iCloud on Your Computer

As we mentioned earlier in this chapter, iCloud works both with iOS devices and computers that run Windows or OS X. So, even if your iPhone is your only iOS device, you may find it worthwhile to set up iCloud on your computer as well.

On a Mac, iCloud can synchronize Safari bookmarks and reading lists, contacts, calendars, notes, and reminders with your iPhone, and it can instantly upload photos you take with your iPhone either to iPhoto or Aperture, and vice versa, with Photo Stream. In addition, Mac applications that have been designed to work with iCloud can share documents with some iPhone apps. The iCloud System Preferences window (shown next), which is available via the Mac's System Preferences, is where you set up iCloud access on your Mac.

With Windows Vista and later versions of Windows, iCloud can synchronize bookmarks with either Safari or Internet Explorer and can synchronize contacts, calendars, and tasks with Outlook 2007 and later versions. It can also copy images from your Photo Stream into your Pictures folder. What's more, both Macs and Windows computers running iTunes can take advantage of automatic downloads of music, apps, and books.

All recent Macs running Mac OS X 10.7.4 or later already include all the necessary software to run iCloud; on Windows computers, on the other hand, you must download both the iCloud control panel (similar to the iCloud System Preferences window on a Mac) and iTunes from Apple to take advantage of iCloud. In either case, complete instructions for setting up iCloud on your computer, as well as the software you need to install iCloud on Windows, are available from Apple at www. apple.com/icloud/setup/.

Use Other Cloud Services

Of course, iCloud is neither the only nor the first cloud service. There are many others, including some designed for very special purposes and others that are quite broad in scope. We can't hope to describe the wide array of cloud services that you can access with your iPhone, but, instead, we offer a brief look at two popular services to give you a sense of what's available: one service that, like iCloud, provides a number of different capabilities and features, and another service that has a much more narrow focus.

Use Google

If you have spent any time on the Internet at all, you have probably used the Google search engine. In fact, so popular is Google for searching that its name has come to be used as a verb; for example, "Last night, I Googled my own name and you won't believe what I found!"

However, Google offers far more than searching capabilities. Elsewhere in this book we've briefly discussed Google's e-mail service (Gmail), a service that also provides contacts and calendars. Aside from those, Google offers a number of other cloud-based services, including document creation and editing, maps, videos, ebooks, photo storage and display, and even language translation.

On your computer, you typically access Google's cloud services from your web browser. However, Google offers a free iPhone app that provides access to most of its services, as well as a number of specialized iPhone apps that each provides access to a specific service. (You can obtain these apps from the App Store, as we describe in Chapter 11.) The main screen of the Google app currently looks like the one shown next—we say "currently" because Google is seldom behindhand in making changes to its offerings.

To see the cloud-based apps Google offers, tap the Apps button near the bottom of the screen. Nothing may seem to happen, but the Google app now knows that you are interested in seeing apps. To actually see them, you then tap the down-arrow symbol in the upper-right corner. The On The Web apps finally appear, as shown here. (Why this confusing two-step process? Ask Google; *we* don't know!)

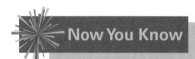

Now You Know — Make Your Own Maps App

In iOS 6, Apple replaced its Maps app with a new version and changed its map data supplier from Google to an assortment of other sources. But if you prefer the way that Google serves up maps, you can make your own Google Maps app using the Google Maps web site.

1. In the Settings app's Privacy settings, tap Location Services, and make sure that it is turned on and that Safari has Location Services enabled (flick down the page to find Safari's entry).

2. Close the Settings app, open Safari, and navigate to maps. google.com.

3. If your iPhone asks you to allow the site to use your location, tap OK.

4. At the bottom of the screen, tap the Share button and, in the choices that appear, tap Add to Home Screen.

5. Change the suggested app name if you like, and then, at the top of the screen, tap Done.

You now have an icon on your Home screen that opens Safari to the Google Maps site when you tap it. (By the way, you can add a bookmark to your Home screen with Safari for any other web page using this technique.)

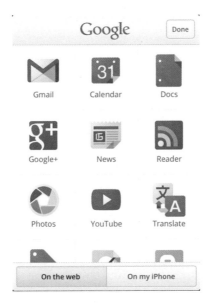

When you tap the On My iPhone button in the Google app, it provides direct links to specialized Google iPhone apps, as shown next. Tap an icon and the Google app switches you to the app you tapped. Note that the apps that the Google app shows may not actually be on your iPhone; if you tap an icon for an app that isn't on your iPhone, the Google app switches to Apple's App Store app so you can obtain it.

Keep in mind that there is nothing to keep you from using both iCloud and Google services on your phone; it's not an either/or choice. In fact, we regularly use both services ourselves, as well as some others.

Use Dropbox

One of the other specialized cloud services that we both use regularly is Dropbox (www.dropbox.com). The service that Dropbox provides (similar to the capabilities provided by other cloud-based services such as SugarSync, Box.net, and CX.com) is a simple one: file sharing between computers and other devices.

When you install Dropbox on your computer, you get a Dropbox folder that looks and acts just like any other folder. However, any files that you drop in that folder appear in the Dropbox folder of any other computer that has Dropbox installed and that uses the same Dropbox account. Furthermore, folders that you create within your Dropbox folder can be shared with other Dropbox users. For example, Dennis can drop the file containing a chapter of this book in a Dropbox folder he shares with Michael, and, when he does this, that file appears almost immediately on Michael's computer in his Dropbox folder. And when Michael edits the file and saves and closes it, Dennis will be able to see the changes the next time he opens that same file on his machine. No e-mail attachments are needed; no special file server needs to be mounted on the desktop. It's just a folder, albeit one that is available simultaneously on several computers at once.

Unfortunately, the iPhone and other iOS devices do not have general-purpose document folders like Macs and Windows computers do. Nonetheless, Dropbox is also handy for iPhone users, because it provides a quick way to get files from a Mac or PC to the iPhone. The next illustration shows what part of the Public folder inside of Michael's Dropbox folder looks like when viewed in the free iPhone Dropbox app.

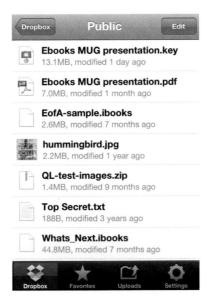

When you tap a file in Dropbox on your iPhone, the Dropbox app attempts to display the file's contents, and that capability works with a wide variety of file types including Word files, PowerPoint files, PDFs, text files, and images, among others. Note, however, that because iOS apps use their own storage and not general-purpose document folders, you can only display the contents of Dropbox files or send their data to a specific iOS app.

But even when the Dropbox app can't display a particular type of file, you still have choices: tap the Open In button at the bottom of the Dropbox screen (shown next), and Dropbox tries to find an app on your iPhone that can handle the file.

For example, Dropbox can't directly display EPUB files (EPUB is the format used by ebooks in Apple's iBooks app). However, if you tap an EPUB file in the Dropbox app and then tap the Open In button, you can choose an app that can open the EPUB file and display it, as shown here:

Unlike iCloud or Google, Dropbox is something of a one-trick pony, but the trick it performs is very useful and one that we use almost every day.

Although you can use your iPhone quite productively without making use of any cloud services at all, its Internet connectivity combined with the inventiveness of cloud service and app developers makes for a very powerful combination. It may not be an exaggeration to say that when it comes to the iPhone and the cloud, the sky's the limit.

Part IV

Obtain Digital Media

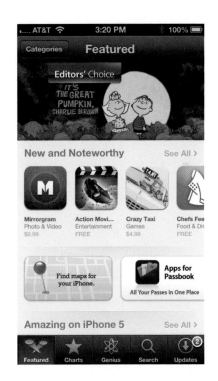

11

Find and Purchase Apps

More than 700,000 apps are available for iOS, and numerous new apps are released every day. There are so many apps for so many purposes that "There's an app for that" has become not just an advertising slogan, but a part of the American vernacular. Some apps are, admittedly, lame, but the vast majority run the gamut from amusing or entertaining through useful, and all the way to "Gee, I wish I'd thought of that!" or "I have to have this app!" In this chapter we'll show you where to go and how to find the apps you want.

Here's an analogy for you: Suppose iOS is a company town and the iTunes Store is the company store. This analogy isn't quite accurate, but it's close. In the case of the App Store part of the iTunes Store, it is spot-on: if you aren't going to "jailbreak" your phone, the only source of apps for your iPhone is the App Store.

 Jailbreaking (removing the protection and restrictions Apple imposes on the iOS software) your iPhone voids your warranty, opens up your phone to malware (Apple vets all software distributed through the App Store as malware-free), results in anomalous behavior in some existing apps, and can seriously impede updating your phone with new iOS releases from Apple. We strongly recommend against the practice, but if you're determined to do it, you're on your own. Additionally, if you jailbreak your iPhone, much of this book won't be that useful to you.

We're not quite certain whether to think of the App Store as a self-contained store in a giant mall called the iTunes Store or to think of the iTunes Store as a huge department store in which the App Store is one of the departments. If you access the iTunes Store via your computer, the department store comparison seems most appropriate (see Figure 11-1). If you want to acquire apps on your iPhone, though, you go through the App Store app and the mall is the more appropriate metaphor. Either works, dependent upon your point of view, so choose one or the other (or both) as your perspective.

Figure 11-1   *In iTunes, access the App Store through the Apps menu.*

Browse and Purchase from the App Store

When you tap the App Store icon on your iPhone, you'll see a screen similar to the one shown next.

We say "similar" because the featured apps are constantly changing as new ones are released and popularity waxes and wanes. Icons along the bottom of the screen let you browse in the five following ways:

- **Featured**   Displays the apps that Apple is currently recommending or promoting
- **Charts**   Displays the most popular commercial apps and free apps, and the top-grossing apps
- **Genius**   Tells the App Store to make recommendations based upon the apps you already have

- **Search**   Lets you search for apps that match user-specified keywords or have the search string as part of their name
- **Updates**   Gives you access to app updates (developers frequently release updates to fix bugs, add features, or just change the look of the app) as well as your purchase history

You can't use Store credit to gift an app at the time we're writing this. Credit card or PayPal information is required. We hope this changes.

Browse Featured Apps

Featured apps appear grouped, as shown in the preceding illustration. At various times, Apple changes the order and headings of the groups. At the time we're writing this, an Editor's Choice is featured at the top, with New and Noteworthy apps appearing next, then some buttons for special purposes (in this case, Maps and Passbook apps), then an Amazing on iPhone 5 header, and then more if you scroll down.

Apple totally revamped the App Store interface while we were writing this chapter and then made subsequent tweaks to the interface before we went to press. The material here is accurate at the time we're writing it and the general drift should still be useful; however, be forewarned that the details are likely to change by the time you read this chapter.

Tap the Categories button at the top of the screen to see the list of app genres displayed next, or a similar list if Apple has added, deleted, or renamed categories between the time we wrote this and the time you're reading it. Note that the listed categories are also in the Apps menu displayed in Figure 11-1.

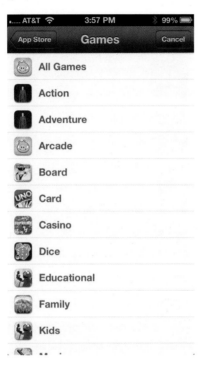

Tap any category to see a list of apps so categorized.

Apps are presented in lists, as shown next, with the icon appearing at the left; the developer name, app name, and rating in the center; and the price (which might be Free) on the right. A small plus (+) sign appears to the left of the price for *hybrid* apps—apps that run at their full resolution on both iPhones/iPod touches and the iPad.

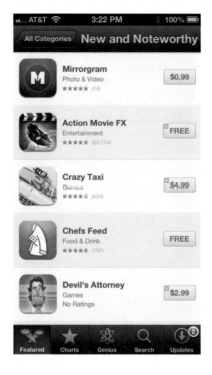

When you tap the name in the list or an app's icon, you'll see the Info screen. If you scroll all the way to the bottom of that screen, you'll see the buttons and information for that app, in the form shown here:

Along the top are buttons that let you view details about the app (Details), the ratings and reviews offered by purchasers (Reviews), and a listing of similar apps (Related).

 Ratings and reviews aren't particularly useful, in our opinions, until a significant number of reviews are available. Further, you should probably focus more on the ratings and reviews for the current version than those for previous product iterations.

Browse Bestsellers

Tap the Charts icon and you can choose among the most frequently purchased apps that have a price tag (Paid), the most often downloaded price-less apps (Free), and the apps that bring in the most revenue

(Top Grossing), as shown next. All three are pretty self-explanatory, but keep in mind that an app that costs $9.99 can sell 1000 copies and gross more than a 99¢ app that sells 10000 copies ($9990 to $9900), so the app's price can have a huge impact on this list's order (and, obviously, free apps don't make it onto the list on their own merit).

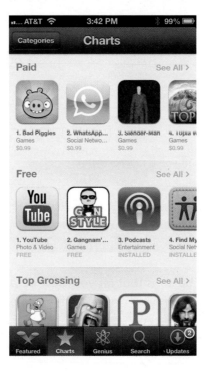

 Actually, there is a way that a "free" app can make it onto the Top Grossing list. "In-app purchases," particularly popular in games, can boost a free app onto the list. The developers of these apps have obviously taken to heart the lesson taught by Gillette and Schick in the 1960s, when they gave away their razors in order to sell blades. Cynics (such as Dennis) might look at free apps that are high-grossers as a warning to stay away, lest their hard-earned money slip out of their hands in the heat of play—your mileage may vary.

Browse Genius Recommendations

Apple is really fond of using the word "genius," both in describing the technical support personnel in its retail stores and in its automated sales recommendations in the various online stores the company operates. Tapping the Genius button initially presents this screen:

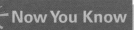 **How Smart Is the Genius?**

Genius is also a topic about which we hold different viewpoints. Michael, whose tastes tend to the more current and popular, thinks that Genius does a pretty good job of making recommendations (particularly in music). Dennis, who tends to be less mainstream and more of a throwback to a previous generation, finds the Genius recommendations close to useless in music and only marginally useful for apps.

Before turning on Genius by tapping its button, we recommend tapping the button at the bottom of the screen to tell you more about the Genius feature. There, you'll learn what information your iPhone sends to Apple and how that information is used.

Browse by Searching

When you have some idea what you're looking for, either because you know the app's name, or you have one or more keywords to narrow down the hits to a few apps or to apps with a specific function, the Search icon is your daddy. Tap it and get a familiar search screen where, when you start typing, a list of matches appears, narrowing the more you type, as shown here:

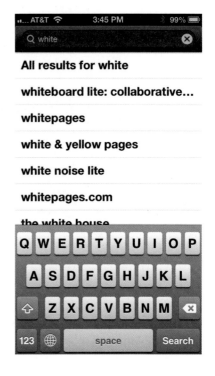

Tap one of the search results and you'll be presented with a horizontally scrolling selection of apps that correspond to the result:

Browse What You Own

Updates, the icon at the far-right on the bottom of the screen, is your avenue to perusing the apps you've purchased and obtaining updates to apps you have installed. Believe us when we tell you that app developers release updates frequently, either to fix bugs, add functionality, or just to make their app prettier or easier to use. (It's a rare day when Dennis doesn't find updates available for at least two or three of his apps, and compared to people he knows, he doesn't have all that many apps.) Tap Updates and you'll see a screen similar to the one shown here:

   You can tap an individual app's name that has an available update to learn more about the update and install it. You can also tap the Update All button at the upper right to start the download and install process for all available updates. Prior to iOS 6, when you started an update, the App Store exited and reverted to the Home screen, where the action took place. Now, however, the download and install process takes place in the background, and you can continue browsing and purchasing in the App Store. (A cynic might advance the idea that this change was to keep you shopping and spending, rather than risk you being distracted while the updates take place and neglecting to go back to give your plastic a workout. We will acknowledge, in counterpoint, that we have more than once entered the App Store to purchase something, seen that updates were available, and decided to take care of them, totally forgetting why we were there in the first place.

So, the change can also be viewed as beneficial by those who have busy lives and get distracted.)

Tap Purchased and you'll see the next screen. The two handy tabs at the top let you scan through all the apps you've purchased (including free apps you've downloaded) via your current Apple ID or just browse through those that aren't present on this iPhone. We discuss Purchased in more detail in the next section.

Restore Purchased Apps

If you have deleted an app from your iPhone, as discussed in Chapter 5, you can restore it to your iPhone at a later time—usually. The exception is when an app is no longer available through the App Store. For example, applications that haven't been updated to work with the current iOS version within a reasonable timeframe get culled by Apple. Similarly, if the developer goes out of business or stops maintaining its product, the app might disappear from the virtual shelf. However, when an app, even a newer version of the app, is still stocked, you can download and reinstall at no charge. Again, there's a caveat: if the newer version incurred an upgrade fee and the version you purchased didn't (rare, but not unheard of, especially for games that were initially released as free), you will be asked to pay the upgrade fee to obtain the new version. The Purchased button in the Updates screen is your gateway to retrieving deleted software as well as software you might have purchased on another iOS device or via iTunes on your computer and neglected to install on your iPhone.

We recommend tapping Not On This iPhone rather than All, just because the shorter list will make it easier for you to locate the deleted software. Tap the Install button to initiate the install immediately after confirming with your password, or tap the app's entry, check out the Info screen, and then tap the Install button.

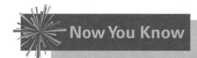

Now You Know — The App Store's Game Center Section

There remains one class of apps that is generally obtained through the App Store by an indirect route. Those are game apps that operate through Game Center, Apple's arcade and social networking venue for gamers, to which you were introduced in Chapter 5. Game Center members can track what their friends are playing, issue invitations and challenges, and discourse on the games they play. Lest you surmise that Game Center is solely the province of pimple-faced and acne-scarred adolescents devoid of interpersonal skills, Game Center offers games for anyone, from small children to senior citizens, and all ages participate. We know of grandparents who use Game Center to play with their grandchildren who might be hundreds (or thousands) of miles away. In that sense, Game Center is a wonderful way to stay connected with distant friends and family. On the other hand, cynics among us (and this includes Dennis, to an extent) believe that Game Center is just a way to promote app sales, bringing revenue into Apple's coffers, and distracts users from more productive pursuits. It's probably somewhere between the extremes.

12

Buy Music, Movies, and TV Shows

When Steve Jobs introduced the first iPhone in 2007, he began by saying that Apple was introducing "a wide-screen iPod with touch controls" and waited a few seconds before mentioning that it was also a mobile phone. That characterization is as true now as it was then: Your iPhone is still a wide-screen iPod with touch controls. With its Music app and Videos app, you can play all the same media that you can play with any other iPod. Plus, you can do all the other stuff we covered in the previous chapters, as well as the stuff we'll describe in the chapters ahead. In this chapter, we'll explain how to use your wide-screen iPod to get music, movies, podcasts, and TV shows from the iTunes Store, along with how to play your media after you get it.

Shop in the iTunes Store

If you have ever shopped in the iTunes Store on your computer, you know about the vast array of entertainment it makes available to you. If you have never done so, you're in for a treat: millions of songs, and tens of thousands of movies and TV shows, not to mention podcasts, audiobooks, and more, are just a tap away.

While iTunes on your computer is both a media player and a portal to Apple's various digital media stores, on your iPhone the iTunes app is only the latter. It's the app you use to buy (or, in many cases, download for free) the media that you play with other apps on your iPhone.

 You must be connected to the Internet via Wi-Fi or a mobile data connection to use the iTunes app.

Sign In to the iTunes Store

You can immediately open the iTunes app and start window-shopping, but if you want to buy anything, you need to sign in with your Apple ID:

1. Open the iTunes app and swipe down to the bottom of the screen to the Sign In button; then tap it. A Sign-In dialog appears, as shown:

2. Do one of the following:

- If you have an Apple ID, tap Use Existing Apple ID, and then enter your Apple ID and password.

- If you don't have an Apple ID or want to create a new one to use just for iTunes purchases, tap Create Apple ID, and follow the prompts.

Apple uses the credit card number associated with the Apple ID you use when you sign in for any purchases you make in the iTunes Store. If you don't have an associated credit card, you are asked for this information when you attempt to make a purchase.

 **Viewing and Managing Your iTunes Account Settings**

To find out which Apple ID you signed in with and manage its settings, swipe to the bottom of the screen. Instead of the Sign In button, you'll see the current Apple ID being used. Tap it, and then, in the dialog that appears, tap View Apple ID. When you enter your password, you'll see the Account Settings screen.

On the Account Settings screen you can manage various settings, such as the current Apple ID being used, the password, the credit card you use for purchases, subscriptions to various types of media such as multi-pass TV purchases (see "The TV Shows Store" later in this chapter), and other account-related information. Tap Done at the top of the Account Settings screen when you are finished viewing or making changes to your settings.

You can also sign out and in to an iTunes account with the Settings app: Tap iTunes & App Store, and then, at the top of the screen, tap the current Apple ID. (If you are already signed out, you'll see a Sign In button at the top of the Store settings screen.)

The Stores in the iTunes Store

When it was first introduced, the iTunes Store was just that: an online music store. Over the years it has grown from a simple music store to a sprawling online media mall, offering all sorts of digital wares. You'll find a Music store, a Movies store, a TV Shows store, an Audiobooks store, and a Tones store.

The Music Store

When you open the iTunes app, the bottom of the screen shows a favorites bar with the Music icon at the far left, as shown—unless, of course, you have changed it (see "Configure Your Favorites" later in this chapter). Tap the Music icon to enter the Music store. This store is, unsurprisingly, the one you want for music, including music videos.

At the top of the Music store screen are buttons, shown next, that give you different ways of accessing the store's wares:

- **Featured**   Tap this to access the main sales screen for the Music store, which presents featured new releases at the top. Below those are various categories of music releases: albums and EP collections, singles, not-yet-released items available for preorder, other specials, and free items, including a free "Single of the Week." Tap any one of the items listed to get more information, and tap an individual song to hear a sample.

- **Charts**   Tap Charts to access a screen that presents various lists of top-sellers: songs, albums, and music videos, as shown next. Flick through each list to see the current top-sellers in the store.

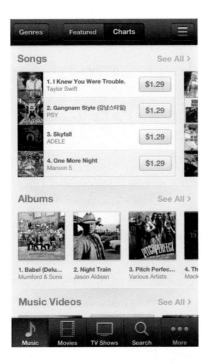

- **Genres** This screen lists the various genre categories for the store, such as blues, classical, dance, and so on. The Genres button works in conjunction with the Charts and Featured buttons. For example, if you tap Charts, tap Genre, and then tap Blues in the list of genres, you see the top-selling blues items in the iTunes Store; if you tap Featured, tap Genre, and then tap Blues, you see the featured blues items. Tap All Genres at the top of the Genres list to see everything.

- **The list icon button** Tap this button on the far right to see a history list that shows you the most recent items you have viewed in the store.

The Movies Store
The Movies store offers theatrical as well as direct-to-video movies. Similar to the Music store screen, the Movies store screen, shown here,

offers new and noteworthy movies, special offers, and other categories to shop:

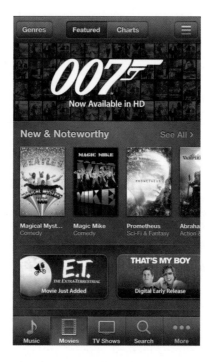

The buttons along the top of the screen provide the same functions for movies that they do for music: you can view featured movies, movies listed by top sales and rentals, and either featured or top-selling movies within a particular genre.

Just as you can hear song samples in the Music store, you can see a trailer for any movie, and if one takes your fancy, you can either buy or rent it—or both, as shown here:

When you rent a movie, you can keep it, unwatched, for 30 days; once you begin to watch it, you have 24 hours (in the United States; other international iTunes Stores have different time limits) to finish viewing it (and even watch it again) before it disappears from your iPhone. (See "Rules for Movie Rentals" later in this chapter.)

The TV Shows Store

The TV Shows store makes both individual TV shows and complete season collections of TV series available for purchase. As with the other stores, you can view featured shows and top-selling shows, and you can winnow them down by genre.

For a currently running series you can buy a *Season Pass*, which downloads individual episodes that have already aired and preorders those that are yet to air; in the case of the latter, you receive each new episode within a day or two following the episode's broadcast. Some ongoing series that are not seasonal, such as talk shows, also offer *Multi-Pass* options that provide a specific number of episodes per purchase. Note that Multi-Pass purchases automatically renew; you must cancel the Multi-Pass in the iTunes Store account settings for the Apple ID you used when purchasing it before it renews. (See "Viewing and Managing Your iTunes Account Settings" earlier in this chapter.)

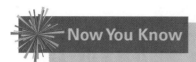

Now You Know — Rules for Movie Rentals

You can rent a movie from the Movies store on your computer, on your iPhone, or some other iOS device, such as an Apple TV. However, different rules apply, depending on the device you use to make the rental:

- If you rent a movie via iTunes on your computer, you can transfer it to another device, such as your iPhone. When you transfer the rental, it disappears from the iTunes library on your computer and moves to the device. If you like, you can move it back to your computer's iTunes library or to another device. In any case, the rental movie appears on only one device at a time.

- If you rent a movie via an iOS device, such as your iPhone, you can view it only on that device. You cannot transfer it to another device or to your computer.

Therefore, for maximum flexibility, we advise that you rent movies through iTunes on your computer unless you are sure you want to watch it on a particular iOS device.

Audiobooks, and Tones

In addition to the Music, Movies, and TV Shows stores available by default on the favorites bar at the bottom of the iTunes app's screen, two other stores are available: the Audiobooks store and the Tones store. To see them, tap More at the right end of the favorites bar:

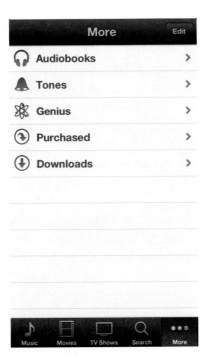

Each of these stores subdivides its offerings into featured, charts, and genres just as the Music store does (although the Audiobooks store calls genres "categories").

- **Audiobooks**   Before the advent of iPods, these were known as *books on tape*: published books read aloud that you could listen to on a portable music player instead of reading them yourself. The Audiobooks store offers thousands of audiobooks in a wide variety of categories that you can purchase and download to your iPhone: perfect for when you want to listen to a new bestseller or an established classic during your morning commute or while you're walking the dog.

- **Tones**   Tones is short for ringtones—the sound that plays when your iPhone rings (in Chapter 6 we described how to assign and use them). Many performers make small samples of their work available in ringtone format for you to purchase and use on your iPhone, and the Tones store is where you buy them.

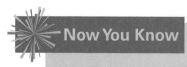

About Podcasts and the Podcasts App

Podcasts are shows akin to radio and TV shows that are made for digital distribution and that are, in most cases, organized as episodes in a series. They cover a wide gamut of topics and genres and a wide assortment of running times as well. Both video and audio podcasts are available. Using iTunes on your computer, you can subscribe to podcast series and have new episodes download to your iTunes library so you can sync them to your iPhone, or you can use Apple's free Podcast app, available in the App Store, to subscribe to them and download them directly to your iPhone. (See Chapter 11 for more on obtaining apps from the App Store.) The podcasts provided by Apple are free, so feel free to sample as many as you like.

A relatively recent addition to Apple's collection of free apps, the Podcasts app lets you search Apple's Podcast store for podcasts, download individual podcasts, subscribe to podcast series, and play podcasts. In addition, the app also lets you play Internet radio stations that provide free audio streams from around the world.

You don't need to use the Podcasts app to play podcasts: if you don't have the Podcasts app, you can sync any podcasts to which you subscribe in your iTunes library to your iPhone and play with the Music app. However, if you become addicted to podcasts (and we know several people who are), you owe it to yourself to download the free Podcasts app from the App Store and see if it suits you. Personally, we find its retro-styled tape-recorder interface worth a look just for its amusement value.

Genius and Downloads

The other default items on the More screen of the iTunes app are something of a hodgepodge. Here's a brief summary of what they do.

- **Genius** This feature helps you find items in the iTunes Store that that you might like based upon items you have already purchased. It offers separate screens for music, TV shows, and movies. You can purchase items directly from the Genius screens.

- **Downloads** If you have made any media purchases but not yet downloaded them (say, for example, you purchased a movie but didn't have Use Cellular Data turned on in the iTunes & App Stores settings in the Settings app), you can find them listed on this screen and download them when you have a Wi-Fi connection.

Searching the Store and Viewing Purchases

As much fun as it is simply to shop in the various stores inside the iTunes Store, sometimes you know exactly what you want and you just want to get to it without having to swipe through several screens. That's what the Search button on the favorites bar is for.

Tap the Search button and you'll see a search field appear at the top of the screen; the iPhone keyboard appears so you can type your search. As you type, the app suggests items that match what you have typed so far, as shown:

You can flick through the list of suggestions and tap the one you want, or, if none of the suggestions are quite what you want, tap the Search key on the keyboard to search for everything that matches what you have typed.

When you complete a search by tapping either the Search key or a suggestion, the iTunes app presents the results of the search, as shown. The search shows you the matching results for all the stores, or you can narrow it down to individual types of media using the buttons along the top of the screen: tap the More button to select media from a particular store.

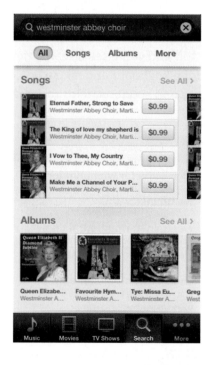

You can then tap an item in the search results to get more information about it or to hear or see a preview. If the item shows a price (or is marked as Free), tap the price button or the Free button to obtain the item.

19	**Be Strong and of Go...** Westminster Abbey Ch...	2:06	$0.99
20	**I Vow to Thee, My C...** Westminster Abbey Ch...	2:28	$0.99
21	**Orb & Sceptre March** Martin Baker	8:41	$0.99
22	**Fanfare & National A...** Westminster Abbey Ch...	2:16	$0.99

To perform a new search, tap the gray X at the right of the search field and type something else. You can also tap within your search term and type again to edit and refine it.

What if you see an item in one of the stores and you're not sure whether you already own it? Rather than relying upon your memory, or switching out of the iTunes app to search your music or other media collections, you can tap More on the favorites bar and then tap Purchased. The iTunes app offers you media category buttons corresponding to the stores available through the iTunes app, as shown:

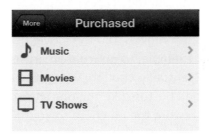

Tap one of the buttons to see a screen of items that you have purchased in that store. You can view every item that you have purchased in that store, as shown, or only those items that are not on your iPhone. Music purchases are organized by artist; tap an artist's entry to see individual items by that artist. TV shows and movies are organized by title.

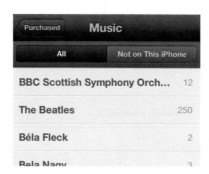

Viewing items that are not on your iPhone is useful if you want to download something you have purchased directly to your iPhone rather than syncing it from your iTunes library on your computer—if it is even in your iTunes library, after all, you can delete purchases from the iTunes library as well. However, the iTunes Store remembers everything that you have bought and can restore any of your previous purchases to your iPhone free of charge.

To download an item, tap the artist's name to see individual songs by that artist; for TV shows, tap the title of a show to see individual seasons and episodes; for movies, tap the movie title. You may have to tap several times, for example, to go from an artist to an album to a song on the album. Eventually, though, you get to a screen that has a cloud-shaped download button, like the one shown here. Tap that download button to restore the purchase to your iPhone.

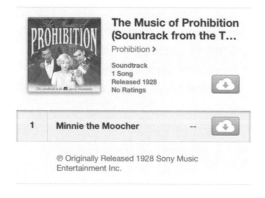

Configure Your Favorites

You don't have to settle for the default arrangement of buttons on the favorites bar at the bottom of the iTunes app screen if you don't want to. For example, if you don't plan to watch many videos on your iPhone but have a penchant for audiobooks, you can swap the Audiobooks button for the Videos button. The only button that you can't move or replace is the More button.

Here's how to arrange your favorites as you like:

1. Tap More on the favorites bar, and then, on the More screen, tap the Edit button on the screen title bar at the top. The Configure screen, shown next, appears:

2. Do any of the following:

   • From the collection of buttons in the top half of the screen, drag a button over a favorites bar button and then lift your finger. The button on the bar over which you drag the new button lights up, as shown, and is replaced by the new button when you lift your finger.

- Drag a button on the favorites bar to a different position on the bar. The bar rearranges itself accordingly.

3. At the top of the Configure screen, tap Done.

Use the Music App

You use the Music app to play your music, audiobooks, and podcasts. (If you don't have the Podcasts app installed, see music and audiobooks. (If you don't have the podcasts installed it will also play those.) Each screen in the Music app shows a particular view of some part of your iPhone's audio collection, such as the Albums screen shown next. Like the iTunes app, the Music app has a favorites bar that you can configure as you like; configuring the favorites bar in the Music app works the same as it does in the iTunes app (see "Configure Your Favorites" earlier in this chapter).

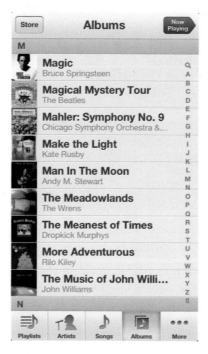

Views of Your Tunes

Even an iPhone model with the least amount of storage that Apple sells is capable of holding thousands of songs and other audio items. Getting to the one you want to play would be difficult if the Music app didn't have a way of organizing your audio for you.

Most of the views that the app offers provide similar layouts and capabilities. For example, they generally present items alphabetically, such as the Artists view shown here; you flick up and down the list to move through it.

Along the right side of the list is a small alphabet column; tap a letter to move quickly to the part of the list that begins with that letter. In addition, a small magnifying glass search icon appears at the top of the right-hand column. Tap that icon to see a search field in which you can enter part of a name or a title; you can also swipe down when at the top of one of the view screens to see the search field. Searches are not limited to the current view: they search your entire audio collection.

Most of the views provide a Now Playing button at the top of the screen so you can browse your audio collection and then return to whatever is currently playing. There is also a Store button you can tap to open the iTunes app so you can buy more media for your iPhone.

Between the buttons on the favorites bar and on the More screen, here are the different views that the Music app provides:

- **Artists**   This view arranges your audio alphabetically by recording artist. Tap any artist entry to see the tracks on your iPhone attributed to that artist. Note that the name of the artist is not necessarily the same as the name of the composer of a piece of music—that's a separate piece of metadata (see "What Is Metadata?" later in this chapter), and the Music app provides a Composers view for just that.

- **Songs**   As far as the Music app is concerned, a *song* is any audio track in your collection other than a chapter from an audiobook or a podcast. The song list includes the name of the artist and the album from which the song came, as shown. Tap any song in the list to play it.

- **Albums**   This view presents the albums in your audio collection, drawn from the metadata associated with each item you have in the collection. You don't need to have downloaded an entire album to your iPhone for the album name to appear; even one song from an album will make the album name appear here. Tap an album entry to see the songs on that album, and then tap a song to play it.

- **Playlists**   These are lists of tracks that you make yourself, either in the iTunes application on your computer or directly on the iPhone (see "Make a Playlist" later in this chapter). Tap the name of a playlist to see what it contains and to play any or all of its contents.

- **Audiobooks**   This view shows you the audiobooks you have in your collection. Tap a book's title to see its individual chapters and play them. If you have no audiobooks, you won't see this view.

- **Compilations**   A *compilation* is typically an album that contains tracks by various artists and is frequently made up of tracks drawn from other albums by its publisher. You can't mark a track as being part of compilation on your iPhone, though you can do so in the iTunes library on your computer. Tap the name of a compilation to see the tracks it contains and to play any or all of them.

- **Composers**   Not all tracks in your audio collection have metadata specifying a composer, but those that have such metadata can be found by using this view. Composers are particularly useful for classical music. For example, the Leonhardt-Consort is the artist that performs the *Brandenburg Concerto Number 6* in Michael's music collection; Johann Sebastian Bach, however, is the composer. Use this view to find tracks by your favorite composers, regardless of the artist performing that track.

- **Genres**   A genre is a type of metadata that can be assigned to a track; it describes the general category to which the track belongs. Typical genres include Rock, Folk, Classical, Comedy, Pop, and Alternative, along with many others. In most cases, the music publisher assigns the genre, but you can create and assign additional genres in the iTunes program on your computer. Use this view to find tracks that belong to specific genres and to play them.

- **Podcasts** If you don't have the Podcasts app installed on your iPhone, your podcasts show up in this list; otherwise, the list doesn't even appear in the Music app. (See "About Podcasts and the Podcasts App" earlier in this chapter for more about podcasts.)

In addition to these views, you can see an entirely different view of your audio collection if you have your iPhone's display rotation unlocked. When you turn your iPhone to landscape orientation, the Music app shows you an album cover view, such as the one shown next. You can swipe left and right to view different album covers, and you can tap a cover to see and play songs from that album.

Make a Playlist

Musical artists and publishers arrange their songs in collections called albums, and the Music app understands those collections and allows you to play them. However, you may want to select just a few songs from an album or make your own collections with tracks drawn from many different albums. These collections, called *playlists*, can be made on your iPhone in the Music app.

Now You Know **What Is Metadata?**

Metadata is data about data. When it comes to a song in your iTunes library or the Music app, the song itself is the data, and the information about the song—its title, performer, genre, length, date of release, how many times you have played it, and so on—is metadata.

When you get a song or other media item from the iTunes Store, it comes with a lot of metadata. The Music app uses the metadata to organize the views that it shows you. With the iTunes application on your computer you can edit a track's metadata (for example, if a song's title or a performer's is misspelled, you can fix it); the Music app on your iPhone, however, does not provide much in the way of metadata management.

Therefore, if you feel the need to fiddle with your music's metadata, we recommend that you sync your audio with iTunes on your computer (see Chapter 9) and manipulate your metadata there. When you sync your audio back to your iPhone, any changes you make to the metadata are included in the sync.

 Adding the same track to more than one playlist does not duplicate the track on your iPhone; playlists simply provide another way for you to organize and play the audio you already have on your iPhone.

To make a new playlist, do the following:

1. In the Music app, tap the Playlists button either on your favorites bar or on the More screen, depending on how you have arranged your favorites bar.

2. On the Playlists screen, tap Add Playlist, and then, in the dialog that appears, type a name for the playlist and tap Save.

3. On the Songs view that appears, tap the tracks you want to add
   to your playlist, as shown. You can also use the buttons on the
   favorites bar and the More screen to select songs from the
   Albums view, Artists view, and so on, and you can use the search
   field in the Music app to find tracks that you want to add. When
   you tap a track, it turns gray so that you know you have added
   it; however, you can still tap it to add it again if you want. (You'll
   see how to remove tracks from a playlist and rearrange the
   tracks in it shortly.)

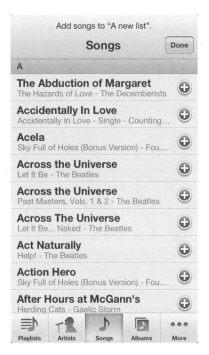

4. When you have finished adding songs, tap Done. The playlist
   appears:

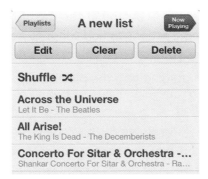

When you view a playlist on your iPhone, you can use the buttons at the top of the screen to edit the playlist, clear the tracks from it, or delete it completely. When you tap the Edit button, you see an editing screen, as shown:

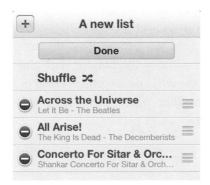

On the editing screen you can do the following:

- **Arrange the tracks**   Drag the drag handle to the right of a track's title up or down to move the track to another position in the list.

- **Delete tracks**   Tap the red circle to the left of a track's title to delete it from the list. Remember that the items in a playlist are only references to the actual tracks in your iPhone's audio collection, so deleting the track in the playlist does not remove it from your iPhone.

- **Add songs**   Tap the + button at the top of the screen. You perform the same actions to add songs to a playlist when you are editing it as you do when you make a new playlist.

When you have finished editing the playlist, tap the Done button above the list.

 In the iTunes application on your computer, you can put playlists inside of folders that can contain multiple playlists. A playlist folder on your iPhone looks like any other playlist in the Playlists view, but when you tap such a playlist folder on your iPhone, it shows the playlists inside of it.

The Music app also offers a special kind of playlist that you can make: the Genius playlist. This feature creates a playlist for you based upon a track that you choose, using information that Apple gleans from the millions of iTunes Store users to make its selections. At the top of the main Playlists view, tap Genius Playlist to create a new Genius playlist: the Music app creates the playlist with the track you tapped as the first selection, as shown, and begins playing it. If you have already made a Genius playlist, tapping Genius Playlist shows you the playlist you created previously.

With an existing Genius playlist you can do the following:

- **Make a new Genius playlist**   Tap New at the top of the playlist to choose a new track and make a playlist based upon it.

- **Refresh the playlist**   Tap Refresh to have the Music app choose a different set of tracks from your audio collection for the playlist.
- **Save it**   Tap Save to give the Genius playlist a name and save it with your other playlists. When you sync your iPhone to iTunes on your computer, that playlist is added to the other playlists in your iTunes library.

Playing Your Tunes

Playing a song on your iPhone is very easy: simply tap a song in the Music app to start it playing. When a song is playing, you can tap the Now Playing button at the top of the screen to see the music playing controls, as shown:

When a track is playing, several sets of controls appear on the screen. The top section, shown next, displays the current track's title, the artist, and the album from which it came. The large arrow at the left, when tapped, goes to the screen you were viewing before you began playing the current track. The list button on the right replaces the album cover

shown on the screen with a list of the tracks on the album from which
the track came.

Below those controls is another set of controls, as shown next. The
top item is the *scrubber bar*; drag the round button, called the
playhead, to move to any part of the song.

Below the scrubber bar is another set of buttons. From left to right,
they do the following:

- **Repeat**   Tap this to replay the current album or list when
  it finishes, tap it again to play the current track again when it
  finishes, and tap it a third time to disable the repeating.

- **Genius**   Tap this to create a Genius playlist based on the current
  song.

- **Shuffle**   Tap this to shuffle the order of songs in the current
  album or list so they play in a different, randomized order.

At the bottom of the playing screen are the *transport* controls and
the volume slider, shown next. Use the volume slider to adjust the
volume of the audio playback. Note that this control also affects the
volume of other applications on your iPhone.

Tapping the leftmost button above the volume slider jumps to the
previous track in the album or list; if you tap and hold it, it acts like a
rewind button. The second button is the *Play/Pause* button: tap it to
start or pause music playback. Tapping the button to its right jumps to
the next song in the album or list; hold it down to use it as a

fast-forward button for the current song. The icon directly to the right of the volume slider is the *AirPlay* icon: if you have another device that can play AirPlay streams, such as an Apple TV, you can choose to send the audio output of your iPhone to that device.

 You can press the iPhone's Sleep/Wake button to put your iPhone to sleep while it is playing and the Music app will continue to play. When your iPhone is playing when the screen is off, you can double-press the Home button to see the play controls. Also, if you are listening with earphones, you can disconnect them and the audio stops playing.

Use the Videos App

Given all the various features and capabilities of the Music app, it is refreshing to turn to the Videos app, which is much simpler by comparison: all it does is allow you to play your movies (including rentals), TV shows, music videos, and video podcasts.

When you open the Videos app, you'll see a screen that lists all of your videos, divided into movies, TV shows, and so on, and arranged alphabetically within each division by title, like the one shown here:

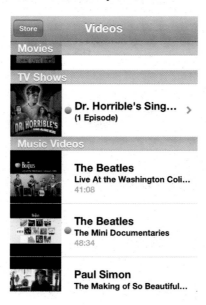

Given that videos take up so much more room than audio tracks (a feature film can take up a gigabyte or more of storage compared to a few megabytes or so for an audio track), chances are that you can fit only a few dozen videos on your iPhone, so you don't need the extensive sorting capabilities for video that the Music app provides for audio tracks.

The main Videos screen offers a Store button in the upper-left corner; tap it to jump to the iTunes app, where you can purchase more media. In the listed movies and videos below the screen's title bar, a blue indicator dot appears if the item has not been played; a half-dot appears for media that has been partially played. For items such as TV shows that may consist of several episodes a > symbol appears to the right of the title; tap the title to see the individual episodes.

Otherwise, tap the title of any video to go to the video playback screen, shown in Figure 12-1. The controls that appear at the top and bottom of the video screen fade out after a few seconds. To make them visible again, tap the video screen. Note that videos always play in landscape orientation, even if you have your iPhone's portrait orientation locked.

Here's what the controls at the top of the screen do:

- **Done button**   Tap this to stop playing the video (the app remembers your playback position) and return to the main Videos screen.

Figure 12-1   *A movie with its video controls showing*

- **Scrubber bar and playhead**   This bar indicates the current playback position in the video, with the time code on the left displaying how much of the video has been played and the one on the right displaying how much time remains in the video. Drag the playhead (the round button in the scrubber bar) to move to a different part of the video. To make fine adjustments, drag down when your finger is on the playhead before you drag left and right: the further down you initially drag, the more fine-tuned your left and right drags become, making it easy to home in on a specific part of a scene. When you drag the playhead, the time codes at each end of the scrubber bar change to reflect the new position of the playhead.

- **Full-screen button**   This double-pointed arrow button can appear at the right of the top controls (not shown in Figure 12-1). Tap it to make the video fill the entire screen from top to bottom and side to side; for some videos, filling the screen may chop off the left and right or top and bottom portions of the frame. Tap the button again to return to the normal view of the video.

Here's what the controls in the control panel at the bottom of the screen shown in Figure 12-1 do (certain controls may not be visible for any given video):

- **Chapters**   The leftmost control appears when a video has internal chapter marks; most video releases of theatrical films have chapters. Tap the control to see the list of chapters, and tap any chapter in the list to go to the start of that chapter in the video. The chapter list also provides a Done button: tap it to return to where you were in the video instead of going to another chapter.

- **Rewind/Previous button**   Tap this to go to the beginning of the current chapter in the video; if a video has no chapters, tapping it takes you to the beginning of the video. Hold your finger down on the button to rewind through the video: the video plays backward at a high speed until you lift your finger from the button.

- **Play/Pause**   Tap this button to pause on the current frame; tap it again to resume playing.

- **Fast Forward/Next**   This works much like the Rewind/Previous button: tap it to jump ahead to the next chapter or the end of the video; hold your finger on it to play the video at a high rate of speed.

- **AirPlay**   This button appears if you have other AirPlay devices (such as an Apple TV) on your local network. Tap it to choose a device and play the audio and video through it. For example, if you have an HDTV and an Apple TV, you can rent a movie on your iPhone and watch it on your TV using the AirPlay capability.

Below the first row of buttons in the control panel are these controls:

- **Volume slider**   Slide this to adjust the playback volume of the video's audio track. It also adjusts the volume setting for other apps on your iPhone.

- **Subtitles**   This button to the right of the volume slider appears if the video has one or more closed-caption tracks. Tap this to see a list of closed-caption tracks, and tap one to make that track's text appear at the bottom of the screen. (Figure 12-1 shows the closed-caption track behind the control panel.)

And that's all you need to know to play videos with the Videos app—except for how to make popcorn, but we'll let you figure that out for yourself.

 In addition to the Music and Videos apps, many other apps can play audio and video material, such as Pandora, Spotify, Netflix, and Hulu Plus. Feel free to explore the App Store for other media apps.

13

Read on Your iPhone

We both got into writing books by chance. By that we mean that authoring was not our career plan. Michael's passion was film, supported by an affinity for computer programming. Dennis's plan was to teach mathematics and programming and develop software. However, we both have been avid readers since early childhood, so much so that our parents searched our rooms for flashlights, headband lamps, and other paraphernalia we used to read under the covers after "lights out." (By the way, luminescent strips don't provide enough illumination to read by.)

If we had the iPhone 50 (plus) years ago, none of that would have been necessary. Nor would we have needed to seek storage for our various books and magazines. One book, or one thousand books and a couple hundred magazines, takes up the same amount of space and weighs the same amount on the iPhone, which stores all your media together in one handy place. Plus, the iPhone provides its own adjustable light source.

 Although the iPhone is a great medium for electronic reading, the iPad is even better, and you can synchronize what you're reading between the two devices with virtually no effort on your part. Talk about the best of both worlds: the iPad for leisurely reading and the iPhone for reading on the go.

Of course, if we had the iPhone back in the 1950s, we also wouldn't have had to deal with extension phones in the bedroom, kitchen, and den; waiting for others in the house to finish their phone calls; long cords if we wanted or needed to move around while on the phone; and a myriad of other conveniences that we now take for granted.

Use iBooks and the iBookstore

When Apple announced the iPad, the company also announced *iBooks*, a reader app for electronic books (ebooks). Close to the time the iPad shipped, it became apparent that, contrary to early expectations, iBooks was not going to be pre-installed but would be a free download from the App Store and would also be available for use on the iPhone and iPod touch.

Between the releases of the iPad 2 and the third-generation iPad, Apple announced the availability of iBooks 2. The most significant feature of iBooks 2, the support for interactive books (primarily textbooks), is restricted to the iPad, so we aren't going to discuss the interactive ebooks further here other than to ask, "Wouldn't it be nice to read them on the iPhone, too?"

Use iBooks

In typical Apple fashion, iBooks is cleanly designed and simple to use. Also, in typical Apple fashion, a few not-so-common capabilities exist that aren't completely obvious on the surface. We're going to assume that you have already downloaded and installed the free iBooks app. If not, do so now. (See Chapter 11 if you don't know how to obtain apps from the App Store.)

Manage Collections

When you first launch iBooks, you're presented with a screen showing what appears to be a bookcase, as shown next. At the top of the bookcase is a toolbar with three buttons: Edit, Books or PDFs (depending upon what's on the shelves), and Store. Just below the toolbar is a Search box, accompanied by two buttons that allow you to switch between the bookcase view (the leftmost button) and a list view of the titles in your Books collection.

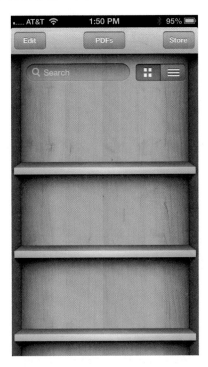

That's right—it's the Books *collection*; the Books button is a label showing which collection is being displayed. iBooks comes with two pre-installed collections, Books and PDFs, but you can add more of your own collections by tapping a collection name to see the Collections screen, shown next, and manage your collections. Tap New at the bottom of the Collections screen to—what else—add a new collection. Tap Edit to rename, reorder, or delete collections (though you can't delete or rename the Books or PDFs collections). To switch to a

particular collection, tap the collection name. Tap Done when you're
finished.

 You don't have to visit the Collections screen to switch the
collection you're using. Swiping left-to-right or right-to-left
switches you to the previous or next collection, respectively.

Read and Navigate

Tap a book on the bookshelf or in the list, if that's how you're viewing
your collection. After a slight animation, the title opens to the last page
viewed, or to the first page if you have yet to start reading the book.

Now You Know   iBooks' Collections

Originally, iBooks didn't offer collections. Instead, your bookcase grew vertically to accommodate as many books (or PDFs) as you added. Obviously, as the bookcase elongated, you had to scroll more to get to a desired title. As usage became more cumbersome, Apple came up with the collection approach, letting you subdivide your library into multiple bookcases of whatever height was necessary to accommodate what you placed in the collection.

One rationale for segregating ebooks and PDFs as separate collections is that the reading experience is different for ePub books (the open ebook format that iBooks recognizes) and PDFs. ePubs reflow the pages based upon the typeface and size you select and whether you are reading in portrait or landscape orientation. PDFs are fixed pages in which you scroll around or zoom out or in.

Some users create collections based on genres—such as mysteries, thrillers, biographies, sci-fi, romance, and so on. Others create separate collections by author, by the first letter(s) of the book title (such as A–C, D–F, and so on), or by personal "star" or favorite ratings. How you choose to organize your collections, other than the two defaults, is totally up to you.

The first page you see could be the book's cover, its table of contents, its copyright page, the first page of the content, or whatever else the publisher chose to make the default when you open the book.

You'll see a row of dots with a slider box at the bottom of the page, as shown next. The dots are the scrubber bar, and you use these along with the box to navigate to various pages within the book. If you don't tap one of the dots within a few seconds, they fade away. Tap in the center of the screen if you want them to reappear.

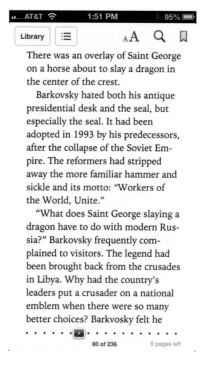

Several buttons appear at the top of the page:

- **Library**   Tap this to go back to the collection in your library.
- **Table of Contents**   Tap this to see the table of contents page, where you can access the table of contents, any bookmarks you've set, and any notes that you've created,

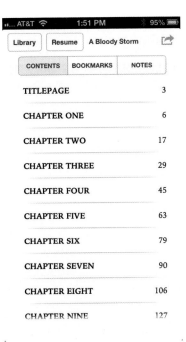

- **Fonts**   Tap this button to change the screen brightness, the font size (small *A* and large *A* buttons), typeface used (Fonts button), as well as the Theme. There are currently three themes–Normal, which is black text against a white background; Sepia, which is dark text against a light brown background; and Night, which is white text against a black background–in iBooks 3 is the option of reading the book in Book mode, which is the traditional page view, and Scroll mode, which presents the contents in a continuous vertically scrolling form.

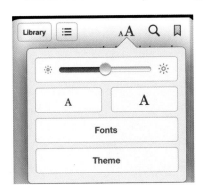
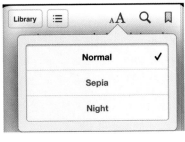

- **Search** Tap the hourglass to open a search page to search the book for specific text.

- **Bookmark** Tap the bookmark icon to place a bookmark on the current page (a small red ribbon appears at the top right of the page).

Drag the box along the row of dots at the bottom of the page to see where you are within the book. Use the slider to scroll to a specific page or position.

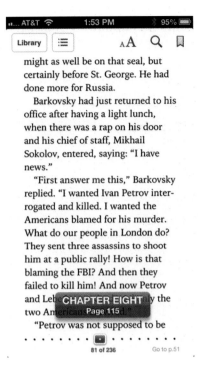

To go to the next page, tap the right edge of the page, or, if you prefer the visual page turning animation to be under your control, drag the right edge to the left. To go back to the previous page, tap or drag the left edge of the page.

iBooks also supplies a set of highlighters, a dictionary, and a thesaurus, and it lets you make the digital equivalent of margin notes, in addition to the expected ability to copy and share text passages.

When you tap a word in the book, iBooks selects the word and displays a toolbar, as shown here. You can resize the selection by dragging the little handles at either end.

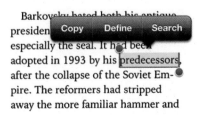

Tap Copy to store the text for pasting in another app (such as Mail or Notes) or in a note you create, similar to writing in the margin of a printed book. Tap Define to look up a word in the bundled *Oxford American Dictionary*, as shown next. Tap Highlight to use the virtual highlighter and emulate a yellow highlighter.

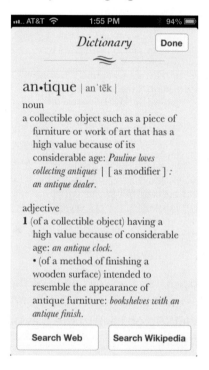

If you're holding the device in portrait mode, tap the right-pointing arrow to see the other toolbar options (you see all of the toolbar options by default in landscape orientation), Note and Search, as shown next. Tap Note to insert margin notes that are linked to the selection. Tap Search to search the book for a word or group of words, as shown at right.

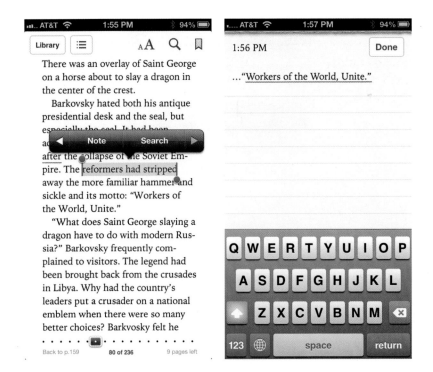

 In landscape orientation, all of the toolbars are combined into one, but we don't know anyone who actually uses iBooks in landscape orientation on an iPhone because of the amount of page-turning involved.

Tapping a highlighted passage presents the toolbar shown at the top in Figure 13-1, which displays the current highlight color with a circle around it, a slashed circle to remove the highlight, and a balloon to take you to the Notes screen. Tap the current highlight color and you'll see the toolbar at the bottom of Figure 13-1, where you can change the highlight color to one of five different colors or underline the text instead of highlighting.

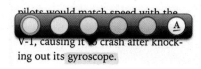

Figure 13-1 *The Highlight toolbar (top) and the Highlight Style toolbar (bottom)*

 The arrow at the right end of the top toolbar in Figure 13-1 lets you choose to Copy, Define, and Search, but it doesn't include a direct way to get back to the highlighting choices. We think this is a design oversight, but it has been this way through a number of releases, so we must assume that Apple has reasons for this, even if we don't recognize the reasons. Just tap the highlighted passage again if you want to return to the highlighting toolbar.

Shop the iBookstore

iOS devices are media consumption tools, and ebooks is one of the media types. Never one to forgo combining a useful feature with a revenue opportunity, Apple created a department within its iTunes Store for electronic books. In iTunes on your computer, click Store in the Source List and then click the Books tab at the top of the content pane. On your iPhone (and other iOS devices), you open iBooks and tap the Store button at the right end of the Library screen's top toolbar.

Once you're in the iBookstore, you'll experience the same familiar environment you enjoy when shopping for apps, music, or video. The typical toolbar for browsing appears at the bottom of the screen, adjusted for a book-buying experience. The first icon on the left represents books and presents the typical Featured and New Releases displays, as shown.

The next icon presents the charts of most-popular titles at the iBookstore (divided into Paid and Free groupings) and the New York Times Bestseller lists, both Fiction and Nonfiction titles.

The third icon, Top Authors, presents a long alphabetized list of the most popular authors for both paid and free titles, as shown. The last two icons are the familiar Search and Purchased icons that function just as they do for music, video, and apps.

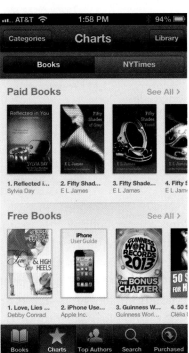

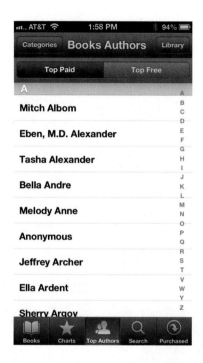

When you tap a book title or image, the book's Info screen appears. Beneath the price (or free) button is a Sample button. If you tap Sample, an excerpt from the book immediately downloads to your Library. You can check out the sample and, if you decide you want the book, you can make an in-app purchase. (Or you can go back to the iBookstore and purchase it there, but we think you'll agree that an in-app is easier and faster.) Near the middle of the screen, below the buttons and metadata (for example, how many books have been sold and the cumulative rating), are buttons for Details (usually a synopsis from the

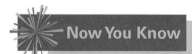 **Now You Know**   **eBook Portability Considerations**

Non-interactive ebooks in iBooks are formatted using an open standard called *ePub*, which stands for electronic publication. Although iBooks can open and display any ePub-formatted book (that doesn't include another company's copy-protections), the titles

available through the iBookstore cannot be read in other ePub readers, such as Nook, Bluefire, or Stanza, due to Apple's DRM (Digital Rights Management) encoding—legalistic terminology for copy-protection code. If you are going to read your ebooks on an iOS device only, the DRM is not an impediment; however, if you might also want to read your ebook on a personal computer, you're out of luck because Apple hasn't produced an ebook reader for those platforms and hasn't licensed the decoding algorithm to any ebook reader publisher for other operating systems. The DRM (which Apple calls *FairPlay*, a misnomer in our opinion) is the primary reason that we seldom purchase our ebooks from the iBookstore, but you might not feel the same constraint; there is a wealth of great content available there, and a fair amount of it is free.

If, however, you're looking for other sources of compatible content, you can find them at a number of web sites. The Project Gutenberg web site (www.projectgutenberg.com) includes links not only to its free ebooks but to books on other sites, such as Google Books and ebooks.com. Most of these titles are either self-published or books for which the copyright has expired; some titles still have an active copyright, but the copyright holder has released the content for free distribution.

One of our favorite sites is the Baen Free Library (www.baen.com/library), a wonderful source of current and recent science fiction offerings from Baen Books. Most Baen hardback titles also include an optical disc with a broad selection of its titles in various formats, among them ePub, PDF, and HTML; not all of these are in their free library—an added inducement to purchase their books. A Google search for "free epub" returns a plethora of sites, many of which have both free titles and purchasable, but DRM-free, titles (such as www.epubbooks.com).

If you're a frequent user of public libraries, most of those institutions provide ebooks, usually encoded with AdobeDRM. iBooks, Stanza, and Nook won't display them, but the excellent Bluefire app will.

publisher), Reviews (customer feedback and includes ratings), and
Related (usually other books by the same author), as shown next:

 We take the reviews with a grain of salt, just like the ratings. This
is especially true of the really negative reviews and ratings that
don't have much company, because they tend to be rants that
don't come across as really pertinent, but your mileage may vary.

Understand the Newsstand

The Newsstand icon on your Home screen doesn't start an app, but opens
like a folder on your Home screen. Be aware, though, that it is a folder
with special features and specific purpose. Newsstand's raison d'être is to
collect and display apps for periodicals—magazines, journals, and
newspapers—to which you subscribe or, at least, in which you can read
individual issues you've purchased. When open, Newsstand resembles a

section of the bookcase familiar from iBooks, but rather than book covers, you see newspapers and magazine covers representing the periodicals you've purchased (including free issues), as shown:

Each periodical image is the icon for the app (such as *The New York Times*) that, when tapped, opens the reader for that publication. Each app is different, tailored to express the publisher's presentation and focus. What each has in common is that although they are almost all free, they all provide a venue to purchase individual issues, subscribe for a number of issues, and allow you to read the publication; purchases and subscriptions generally have a price tag attached.

Use Other Reading Apps

iBooks and the periodical apps that you keep in Newsstand aren't the only reading apps for the iPhone, but they're the apps that Apple provides, or, in the case of Newsstand, the apps that periodical publishers provide.

Amazon's Kindle wasn't the first eReader, but it was the first one to gain popular traction. Since then, Amazon has made software versions of Kindle available for most computer operating systems and handheld devices. Needless to say, the Kindle app for iOS interfaces with Amazon to make your library of Kindle books available on your iPhone. Kindle titles use MOBI (Mobipocket) and AZW formats rather than ePub.

Barnes & Noble, the last remaining major brick-and-mortar bookseller in the United States (a few regional chains remain, but Barnes & Noble is the only nationwide chain still in operation), also has an eReader device called the Nook. Like Amazon, B&N has developed a software platform that allows its books (which use ePub format) to be read on different computer operating systems and mobile devices, including iOS.

Stanza was a widely distributed freeware app for reading ebooks from a group named Lexcycle. In 2009, Amazon acquired Lexcycle and Stanza. Not tied to any one distributor or publisher, Stanza reads a wide variety of formats, including ePub, MOBI, Lit (Microsoft), eReader, PalmDoc, MS Word, RTF, PDF, and HTML, among others.

 Another really well-regarded app is Bluefire Reader. This free app handles ePub and PDF but also provides support for the Adobe DRM used extensively by public libraries for their ebooks.

For fans of comic books and the graphic novel, most major publishers have dedicated apps for their products, which include in-app purchases and subscriptions: DC, Marvel, IDW, Dark Horse, and numerous others. Each of these apps, however, is a closed system in that you can use them to read only what you purchase from their stores, although you can share your account from those stores on multiple devices, including Mac and Windows computers. Dedicated comic readers such as Bookman Pro ($2.99, MobiRocket) and ComicBookLover (free, Bitcartel) let you copy your collection of digital comics from your computer to your iPhone.

Dennis has a huge collection of scanned comic books from his youth—DC primarily, and some Marvel and Gold Key—and is torn between the two apps. He finds the reading experience a bit better in Bookman, but prefers the organizational tools for handling his collection better in ComicBookLover, especially its integration with his master database on a Mac on his home network. You can't really fit more than 300GB on an iPhone, after all.

Part V

Use the Cameras

14

Shoot and Edit Photos

This is a photography truism: the best camera is the one you have
with you. Happily, when you have your iPhone with you, your best
camera is a darn good one. Although it may not the rival high-end
cameras that professional photographers and dedicated amateurs
carry around, the iPhone camera has come a long way from the murky
fixed-focus point-and-shooters that were included on early mobile
phones. Sporting a built-in flash, autofocus, face recognition
capabilities, and a wealth of other features, your iPhone is fully able
to capture scenic wonders, detailed portraits, and once-in-a-lifetime
shots—and then share them immediately with your friends, relatives,
and Facebook and Twitter followers. In this chapter we'll show you
how to compose and take striking pictures with your iPhone's Camera
app, and view, edit, and show them to the world with the Photos app.

Taking Pictures with the Camera App

The whole point of a point-and-shoot camera is that it is easy to use:
you don't need to know an f-stop from F. Scott Fitzgerald to use one.
Just point the camera, press the button, and you have a picture. That's
the idea behind the iPhone camera, too.

Shooting Basics

There are two ways to launch the Camera app. The first way is the
traditional way: Tap the Camera app icon on your Home screen. That's

easy enough when your iPhone is already awake, but you can get to the camera even when it's sleeping. That's a great convenience if your iPhone is sleeping in your pocket when the photo opportunity of your dreams is unfolding before you! Here's how to get to the Camera app on a sleeping iPhone:

1. Press either the Home button or Sleep/Wake button on your iPhone.

2. On the lock screen, to the right of the Slide To Unlock slider, slide the camera icon, shown here, up. The lock screen slides up and displays the Camera app.

 You can get to the Camera app from the lock screen even if you have a passcode protecting your iPhone. However, only the Camera app and the images you take are available while your iPhone is locked; the rest of your data is still safe until you unlock the iPhone.

When the Camera app opens, you see a brief image of a closed camera shutter as the app pulls itself together; then, in a second or less, the screen shows the image from the camera lens: the screen acts as your viewfinder. The camera controls appear along the bottom of the screen if the iPhone is held in portrait orientation, as seen in Figure 14-1, or along the side if the iPhone is held in landscape orientation.

Here's what the controls shown in Figure 14-1 do:

- **Last picture**   This button, at the left of Figure 14-1, shows a thumbnail of the last picture taken; tap it to open the Photos app so you can review the picture, as shown (additional buttons to the ones shown here may appear at the bottom of the screen

Figure 14-1   *The Camera app controls*

as well). You can delete the picture if it came out badly by
tapping the Trash button at bottom right, and return to the
Camera app by tapping the blue Camera button at bottom left.
(We describe some of the other capabilities of the Photos app
later in this chapter.)

- **Shutter**   Tap the button shown at the center of Figure 14-1
  to take a picture. Instead of tapping, you can hold your finger
  down on the button until you are ready to take the shot; when
  you lift your finger the picture is taken. Notice that an
  animation shows the picture in the viewfinder portion of the
  screen jumping into the last picture thumbnail when you take a
  picture.
- **Camera mode**   Tap the button shown at the right of Figure 14-1
  to switch between using your camera as a still picture camera
  and using it to shoot videos. Shooting video is described in
  Chapter 15.

 In addition to using the on-screen shutter button in the Camera
app, you can take a picture by pressing and releasing the volume-
up button on the side of the iPhone.

Autofocus and Auto Exposure

Your iPhone camera has a powerful computer behind it that enables it
to be very smart about how it focuses and sets exposure. The Camera

app uses facial recognition software to find up to ten faces within the frame, and then it automatically adjusts the exposure setting and the focus to provide the best possible picture to include them all. You'll see one or more blue rectangles in the viewfinder window when the app determines where to focus, such as in the single focus-point example shown here. As you move the camera around to compose your shot, the app continues to adjust the autofocus and auto exposure.

You can, of course, override the facial-recognition–based autofocus and auto exposure for a shot and tell the Camera app where to focus: In the viewfinder, tap the part of the image where you want the app to focus and set its exposure. The blue rectangle pulses briefly. Move the camera to view something else to re-enable autofocus and auto exposure.

Sometimes you may want to set a focus distance and exposure, and then reframe the image before shooting it, or you want to shoot more than one picture using the same settings. You can lock the focus and exposure for a shot by holding down on the viewfinder until the blue rectangle pulses and expands briefly and "AE/AF LOCK" appears on the screen. Tap the screen again when you're ready to unlock autofocus and auto exposure.

The Viewfinder Buttons

Along the top of the viewfinder are three buttons, shown next, which set certain functions in the Camera app.

These buttons provide the following capabilities:

- **Flash** When you tap the leftmost button, several choices appear for controlling the built-in flash on the back of your iPhone: Auto, Off, and On. Tap Auto to allow the app's software to choose when to use the flash, tap Off to tell the Camera app never to use flash for a shot regardless of the lighting, and tap On to use flash with every shot. This last option can come in handy if you want to use fill light on a backlit image.

- **Options** Tap this button to see the settings options shown next, with which you can turn on the HDR (*High Dynamic Range*) and Grid features, or to shoot a panorama shot. (We describe these features in the following three sections.) The Options button changes to read "Done" when the Options settings panel is visible. Tap Done to save your Options settings.

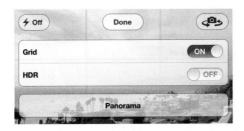

- **Switch cameras** Tap this button at the far right to use the front-facing FaceTime camera on your iPhone instead of the rear camera. This is good for shooting self-portraits, because you can see the viewfinder while composing your shot. Tap it again to switch back to the rear camera.

You can see and use another control, the Zoom control (shown next) by pinching in or out on the viewfinder. Keep in mind that the camera itself does not have telephoto capabilities; instead, when you zoom, the app enlarges each pixel, which can result in blurry images at higher levels of magnification. You can adjust the level of zoom by pinching or by dragging the zoom slider.

Composing with the Grid

The grid, one of the options provided by the Options button in the Camera app, is a time-honored aid to help photographers compose a shot; in fact, the idea behind the grid is older than photography, dating back to aesthetic theories of landscape painting that arose in the late 1700s! The grid helps you visualize what's often called the Rule of Thirds: you divide the frame into thirds horizontally and vertically, and then place your subjects roughly along the lines of the grid, or, for special emphasis, on or near the intersection of the lines (these intersections are sometimes called the "power points"). In addition, the grid provides guidance for where to place contrasting regions of light and dark or of different textures or colors to achieve a harmonious balance between them.

Consider Figures, which show a peaceful autumnal scene and the same shot with a Rule of Thirds grid superimposed on it.

In this landscape shot, one of the tree's lower branches intersects one of the grid's power points, attracting the eye to it and, hence, back up to the dark mass of tree itself, which occupies the top left and left center regions in the grid. The misty distant ridgeline falls along the top line of the grid, confining the lightest part of the shot to the top center and the top right regions; the dark area of reeds fills the regions bounded by the bottom grid line. Finally, isolated in the center region of the grid, just above that bottom line, two fishermen can be seen.

Not every successful picture exploits the Rule of Thirds, and you certainly don't have to use it in your own shots if you would prefer not to. But, if you've never used it before, give the grid a try—it can be surprisingly helpful and it's just a few taps away.

Figure 14-2 *An autumnal scene without grid lines*

Figure 14-3 *The autumnal scene with a Rule of Thirds grid*

Shooting HDR Pictures

The human eye and brain working together make up a very powerful imaging system: you can look at a scene that contains both very bright and very shaded areas and your eye and brain work together to allow you to make out details in both. Cameras are not so flexible: If you adjust the camera exposure to bring out the details in a bright area, shaded areas become almost black; conversely, if you adjust the exposure to bring out the details in the shadows, bright areas become washed out. Take, for example, the following photo. Its exposure is adjusted to show the ocean and the sky above it, but, as a consequence, the shaded bark of the tree and its leaves show little detail, and the grass has a rather dark cast to it.

High Dynamic Range (HDR) images counteract the limitations of single exposure settings by taking several photos in quick succession: one with the standard exposure setting you set with the Camera app, one that is somewhat overexposed to reveal details in the shadows, and one that is underexposed to bring out details in the brightest areas. The multiple photos are then digitally combined by the app to produce images that have lightened shadows and less washed out bright areas, as in the HDR version of the photo you saw previously. In the HDR image, shown next, the texture of the tree bark is now more visible, the leaves have color, and the grass is more vibrant.

There are a few drawbacks to HDR photos, however. For one thing, you can't shoot a series of HDR photos as quickly as you can a series of normal photos, because for each HDR shot, three photos need to be taken, analyzed, and combined. In addition, HDR photos aren't usually suitable for action shots, because the three exposures can cause multiple images of a fast moving object to appear in the combined image, as you can see in the next HDR shot of a jogger. However, when lighting conditions challenge your photographic prowess, your iPhone's HDR capability can sometimes save the day.

 You can choose to keep both the HDR photo and the normally exposed non-HDR version of it. In the Settings app, tap Photos & Camera, swipe to the bottom of the settings screen, and turn on Keep Normal Photo.

Shoot a Panorama

In the old days (that is, the days before iOS 6 and the iPhone 5 came out), you could create a panorama picture by taking several pictures as you slowly swiveled about and then stitching together the separate photos you took using an app like Photoshop. With the iPhone 5, you still have to swivel about, but the Camera app software does all the stitching for you automatically and seamlessly.

Here's how to create a panorama with the iPhone 5:

1. In the Camera app's viewfinder, tap Options, and then tap
   Panorama. The Camera viewfinder displays the panorama
   controls, as shown.

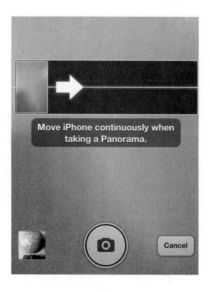

2. Aim the camera at the leftmost point you want to include in the
   panorama and tap the shutter button.

3. *Slowly* swivel from left to right (the Camera app warns you to
   slow down if you turn too quickly). As you move, the arrow in
   the viewfinder's center panel moves from left to right; make
   sure to keep the tip of the arrow on the center line of the panel
   while swiveling. When the arrow reaches the right edge of the
   panel, the complete panorama image jumps into the thumbnail
   area at the bottom of the viewfinder and a Done button
   appears at the lower right of the viewfinder.

4. To take another panorama, tap the shutter button again;
   otherwise, tap Done.

You can tap the arrow in the viewfinder before you start shooting a panorama to shoot the panorama from right to left instead. Also, when shooting a panorama, you can tap Done at any time to finish the panorama at that point.

Here's an example of a panorama photo. Note that panorama photos tend to be large: the original version of the one shown here is almost 17MB in size, with dimensions of 10800×2332 pixels!

Using the Photos App

The Camera app and the Photos app go hand in hand. When you take a picture with your iPhone camera, it ends up in the Photos app's Camera Roll for you to view, edit, and share. But the Photos app is not limited to photos from the Camera app: it also stores photos from other iOS devices via the iCloud Photo Stream, images that you copy from web pages or from e-mails, and the photos that you sync from your computer. Finding your way among the various features and capabilities of the Photos app is key to managing your photos on your iPhone.

The pictures stored within the Photos app are arranged in a number of different ways, each of which you can access from the button bar at the bottom of the Photos app's main screen, as shown.

We describe each of these arrangements more fully later in this chapter, but here's a brief rundown of them:

- **Albums**   With two exceptions, albums are collections of photos that you create. You can create albums on your computer (using a program such as iPhoto on a Mac or by choosing a picture folder on Windows) and then sync those albums with your iPhone, or you can create them directly on your iPhone. The two exceptions are these: the Camera Roll album, which contains all the pictures you have taken with your iPhone, and the Photo Library, which contains all the pictures you have synced from your computer to your iPhone.

- **Photo Stream**   These are synced photos that come from iCloud, including photos taken with your iPhone, photos taken with other iOS devices that use the same iCloud account, and shared Photo Streams from other iCloud users. Some iCloud-savvy Mac programs (such as Aperture and iPhoto) can also put photos in an iCloud Photo Stream; on Windows you can use the iCloud control panel to send pictures to the Photo Stream. We discuss Photo Stream later in this chapter in the section "Sharing and Photo Streams."

- **Events**   Some computer photo applications automatically arrange photos in collections based upon when they were taken; these are known as *events*. You can sync photos from events stored in an image program on your computer to your iPhone; you view photos from those synced events in the Photos app's Events collection.

- **Faces**   Sophisticated photo applications, such as Aperture or iPhoto, can employ facial recognition software to identify people in photos and then collect the photos that show recognized faces into separate groups, one for each person recognized. When you sync photos from your computer with your iPhone, those photos sorted by facial recognition software can be found in the Faces collections.

- **Places**   Many cameras, including your iPhone camera, can include information about the geographic location at which a photo was taken and attach that information to the photo. The Places collections provide you with the capability of viewing photos organized by where they were taken.

Each of these ways of arranging photos in the Photos app, and what you can do with them, is described in the following section.

Using the Camera Roll and Other Albums

The Album collection in the Photos app contains four types of albums:

- **Camera Roll**   This special album contains photos you created on your iPhone by using the camera, screenshots you've made on your phone, and images that you've copied or downloaded from a mail message, a web page, or an app. You can delete photos from the Camera Roll album, but you can't rearrange the order in which they appear, which is determined by the order in which they have been added to the Camera Roll.

- **Photo Library**   This is also a special album and contains photos you have imported from your computer by syncing with your computer. (We cover syncing in Chapters 9 and 10.) You cannot add or delete photos from this album on your iPhone; you can, however, add or remove photos by including or excluding them the next time you sync. The order in which the photos appear in the Photo Library is by their date of creation.

- **Synced albums**   These are albums of photos that you sync to your iPhone from your computer. You cannot add, delete, or reorder the photos in an album on your iPhone; instead, you reorganize the photos in the album on your computer and re-sync.

- **iPhone albums**   These are albums you create on your iPhone. You can add, delete, and rearrange photos in these albums.

To view the albums currently on your iPhone, tap the Albums button at the bottom of the Photos app's main screen. Each album is listed by its name, along with the number of photos it currently contains, as shown here. The Camera Roll and Photo Library albums always appear at the top of the list.

Arranging, Renaming, and Deleting Albums

To arrange the order of the albums in the list, and to rename or delete any iPhone albums, tap Edit at the top of the screen. Gray lines (the *drag handle*) appear to the right of the albums' names for albums that can be dragged in the list: hold your finger down on an album's drag handle and drag up or down to move it in the list, as shown next; lift your finger when the album is where you want it.

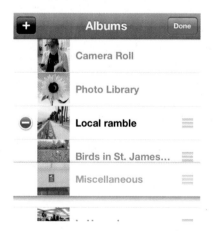

To delete an album, tap the red circle to the left of an album's name—only those albums that you can delete display such circles. When

the Delete button appears beside the album's name, tap it to confirm the deletion.

To rename an iPhone album, tap in its name to get a text cursor, and then use the onscreen keyboard and the iPhone's editing popovers.

When you finish reorganizing your album collection, tap Done at the top of the screen.

Viewing and Arranging Photos in an Album

Tap an album's name to see the photos it contains. The photos appear as thumbnails, like those in the album shown here. If an album contains more photos than can fit on the screen, flick down to see additional thumbnails. To get back to the Albums list, tap Albums at the top of the screen.

Tap any picture thumbnail to view the image it represents. The picture expands to fill the screen, and new buttons appear at the bottom of the screen; note that if you unlock rotation on your iPhone, you can view photos in landscape orientation, as shown here:

You can pinch outward to zoom in on the picture and zoom out by pinching inward. While you are viewing a picture, the buttons at the bottom of the screen fade away, but you can bring them back again by tapping anywhere on the picture. Swipe left and right to view the previous and the next pictures, respectively, in the album. To get back to the thumbnails screen for an album after viewing a photo, tap the button with the name of the album at the top of the screen: if the controls have faded out, tap the photo first to show the controls.

The buttons at the bottom of the screen provide the following capabilities, starting with the leftmost button and moving right:

- **Sharing**   Tap this to choose one of the various ways you can share a photo; we describe photo sharing options in "Sharing and Photo Streams" later in this chapter.

- **Slideshow**   Tap the play button to view your pictures in a slideshow, starting with the picture currently displayed. Before the slideshow begins, you can set the slideshow options (shown next), such as a transition effect to use when the slideshow plays, and whether or not to play music from your audio collection as the show progresses. In the Slideshow Options screen, tap Start Slideshow to begin playing. When the show is playing, tap the screen at any time to stop the show on the currently displayed photo. Note that some other slideshow options can be found in the Photos & Camera setting in the Settings app: whether slideshows loop, how long each picture appears onscreen, and whether the Photos app shuffles the pictures in the album for the slideshow.

- **AirPlay**   This button appears when your iPhone detects an AirPlay-compatible device on your local network. Tap it to choose a device on which to display your photos (such as a large-screen HDTV connected to an Apple TV device). When you have an AirPlay device selected, your pictures appear both on your iPhone and on the AirPlay device; this is a great way to show your photos to a group of friends. Tap the AirPlay button again to choose a different AirPlay device or to turn off AirPlay display of your photos.

- **Delete**   This Trashcan icon appears only in the Camera Roll and in albums that you have created on your iPhone. Tap it to delete the currently displayed photo, and then tap Remove From Album (or, when viewing a photo in the Camera Roll, Delete Photo) to confirm the deletion. Note that removing a photo from an album only removes it from the album but does not delete it from your iPhone; however, deleting a photo from your Camera Roll erases it from your iPhone.

For an album that you created on your iPhone, you can rearrange the photos and remove photos from the album on the album's thumbnail screen. Tap the Edit button at the top of the album's thumbnail screen and then do one of the following:

- **Move a photo within an album**   Hold your finger down on the photo and drag it to a new position, as shown here:

- **Remove photos from an album**   Tap each photo that you want to remove to select it (a checkmark appears on the photo, as shown). Then tap Remove at the bottom of the screen (in the Camera Roll, this button is labeled "Delete"). Then tap again to confirm the removal. Note that photos removed from an album you create on the iPhone are not removed from your phone; they're still present in any other albums in which they appear.

When you finish rearranging or removing photos from an album, tap Done at the top of the screen; if you have made no changes, tap Cancel.

Keep in mind that photos that you delete from the Camera Roll album are removed from your iPhone and from any album in which they appear. The Photos app warns you about this, as shown here:

Creating an Album on Your iPhone

The most important thing you need to understand about albums is that the photos in any album, whether the album was created on your computer or on the iPhone, aren't really *in* the album. The photos are in your Camera Roll or in your Photo Library: any other albums on your iPhone simply show you a custom selection of the photos that are in the

Camera Roll and Photo Library. This means that you can create as many albums on your iPhone as you like, with as many photos in them as you like, without using up your iPhone's storage.

You can create a new album from the main screen in the Albums collection and add photos to it from any album on your iPhone:

1. At the top of the Albums collection main screen, tap the + button.

2. In the New Album dialog that appears, type the name for your new album and then tap Save. A status message appears at the top of the Albums list, as shown:

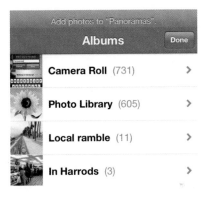

3. Tap any album, and then tap the photos in that album that you want to include in the new album. Checkmarks appear on photos that you tap.

4. To add photos from another album, tap Albums at the top of the screen, as shown, and then, in the Albums list, tap another album and repeat step 3.

5. Tap Done at the top of the screen when you have finished adding photos to your new album. Your new album appears at the bottom of the Albums list.

You can also create a new album, or add photos to an existing album, while viewing the thumbnails of another album:

1. On the thumbnails screen of an album, at the top, tap Edit.

2. Tap the thumbnails you want to add to a new or an existing album. Checkmarks appear on the thumbnails you tap.

3. At the bottom of the screen, tap Add To, and then do one of the following:

   • Tap Add To Existing Album, and then, in the list of albums that appears, tap the album to which the selected photos are to be added.

   • Tap Add To New Album, type the name of the new album, and then tap Save.

 Albums that you create on your iPhone do not sync back to your computer. You can, of course, import photos from your Camera Roll to your computer.

Editing a Photo

You can edit any photo in any album on your iPhone. If you edit a photo that's in the Camera Roll (even if you are viewing it in a different album), those changes appear in the Camera Roll and in all other albums on your iPhone that show the same photo. If you edit a photo that's in the Photo Library (again, even if you are viewing it in a different album) and you save your changes, the Photos app creates a new photo in your Camera Roll that has your changes; the original photo in the Photo Library remains unchanged.

To edit a photo, tap its thumbnail and then tap Edit at the top of the full-screen view of the photo. The editing buttons appear at the bottom of the screen, as shown next. Note that these rudimentary tools are intended only for quick fixes; you can obtain more robust photo editing apps in the App Store.

From left to right, here's what the tools are and what they do:

- **Rotate**   Tap this icon to rotate the photo 90 degrees counterclockwise. Each time you tap it, the photo rotates another 90 degrees.

- **Auto-enhance**   Tap the Magic Wand icon once to have the Photos app make subtle adjustments to the photo. These adjustments usually result in slightly more vivid colors and more dynamic range in muted photos. Tap the button again to turn off the enhancement.

- **Remove red-eye**   When you take a photo using the flash, any subjects looking toward the camera tend to end up with red eyes in the photo, as shown here. This happens because the camera's flash reflects brightly off the retina inside of the eye. Tap this icon to activate the red-eye removal tool. Tap each red eye to remove the redness; you can pinch out to expand the photo to make it easier to tap the red eye. You can undo red-eye removal by tapping the eye again. Tap Apply at the top of the screen when you are done using the tool.

- **Crop**   Tap this icon to crop a photo. A rectangle (displaying the Rule of Thirds grid) appears over the photo, as shown. Drag the corners of the rectangle to change its size and shape; drag the photo to reposition it within the rectangle. Tap Constrain to adjust the rectangle's proportions to one of several different standard proportions, such as 4×3 or 8×10. Tap Crop at the top of the screen to finish cropping the photo; only the portions visible within the cropping rectangle appear in the saved photo.

When you have made all of your editing adjustments, tap Save at the top of the screen. If the photo comes from the Photo Library, tap Save To Camera Roll to finish saving the edited photo in the Camera Roll; otherwise, the changes are immediately saved to the original in the Camera Roll.

 When you save your editing changes, the original photo is still stored in your iPhone, even though it isn't displayed. For example, when you crop a photo from the Camera Roll and save it, you can later edit the photo and readjust the cropping back to the photo's original dimensions.

Sharing and Photo Streams

The Photos app has the capability of sharing your photos in a variety of ways. Earlier in this chapter, for example, you saw how you could share your photos with others using AirPlay and a slideshow. In addition, using the Photos app you can share your photos via e-mail, Messages,

Twitter, and Facebook; you can print photos, assign them to contacts in your Contacts app, and use them as wallpaper for your iPhone's home screen and lock screen. And by using the Photo Stream component of iCloud, you can make your photos available to your other devices and to other people's iCloud-enabled devices; you can even post your photos on the Web for anyone to see.

Share One or More Photos

The key to sharing your photos is the Edit button that appears at the top of any screen of thumbnails in the Photos app, whether they are in an album (described earlier in this chapter), or an event, faces collection, or places collection (keep reading; we describe these a little later).

To share one or more photos, do the following:

1. Tap Edit and then tap one or more photos. Each photo you tap displays a checkmark. Tap a checked photo to remove the checkmark if you decide not to share it.

2. At the bottom of the screen, tap Share. A sharing menu like the one shown here appears:

3. Tap a sharing method.

The number of sharing options that appears depends on the number of photos you select: some options, such as Twitter and Assign To Contact, appear only when a single photo is selected since they accept only one photo at a time. Over time, Apple may add more sharing options to the Photos app, but here's a quick rundown of the ones available in the initial release of iOS 6 and the iPhone 5:

- **Mail** This option creates an e-mail with the photos you have selected attached to it. You can compose a message to go along with the photos and send them to one or more recipients. You can also choose to reduce the size of the attached photos to save space: some e-mail programs cannot accept large attachments.

- **Message** Tap this option to send the selected photos as a message with the Messages app. (We describe that app in Chapter 8.)

- **Photo Stream** To add the selected photos to an existing shared Photo Stream or to create a new shared Photo Stream with the selected photos, tap this sharing option.

- **Twitter** Tap this option to create a tweet with a single selected photo attached to it. You compose the tweet in a panel that appears in the Photos app.

- **Facebook** With this option you can share one or more photos to a Facebook album, along with a caption, which you type in a panel that appears. Tap the name of the album in the Facebook panel to choose a different Facebook album. (By default, the first time you share photos with Facebook from your iPhone, they go into an album named iOS Album; you can rename that album on the Facebook site.) You can also choose who gets to see the photos in Facebook, such as just friends, friends of friends, or everyone.

- **Assign To Contact** Tap this to assign a single selected photo to a contact in your Contacts app. The picture appears when you receive a phone call, e-mail, or message from that contact.

- **Print**   If your iPhone has access to a printer over Wi-Fi, tap this option to print the photos you have selected.

- **Copy**   This is a general-purpose option for selected photos. Tap it to place the selected photos on your iPhone's clipboard so you can paste them within another app, such as a word processing app.

- **Use As Wallpaper**   To use a single selected photo as the wallpaper on your lock screen or Home screen, tap this option.

Share Photos with Photo Streams

Apple uses the name *Photo Stream* to apply to two different, but related, photo services provided by iCloud: My Photo Stream and Shared Photo Streams. If you are signed in to an iCloud account on your iPhone, visit the Settings app, tap Photos & Camera, and then turn on My Photo Stream and Shared Photo Streams to use these services.

My Photo Stream is what Apple used to call Photo Stream in earlier versions of iOS. My Photo Stream copies every new photo you take on your iPhone to your iCloud account on Apple's servers as soon as you join a Wi-Fi network; iCloud then makes those photos available to any iOS device or computer that is signed in to the same iCloud account. The result is that pictures you take on your iPhone appear on your other iOS devices or computers without you explicitly having to sync your iPhone's images. iCloud holds the last 1000 photos you have taken, and the storage used by the photos does not count against your iCloud storage allocation.

You can see the photos in the My Photo Stream collection by tapping the Photo Stream and then tapping My Photo Stream: this is always the first stream listed on the Photo Stream list, as shown in Figure 14-4.

The my Photo Stream screen contains thumbnails of the photos in the stream, just like an album screen, complete with an Edit button at the top. Tap that, tap to select one or more photos, and you see the same buttons you see in an album, as shown next. The Share button brings up the same sharing choices that albums offer, the Save button provides

Figure 14-4   *A list of Photo Streams*

choices for you to save the selected photos either to a new or an existing album, and the Delete button gives you the capability of deleting the photo from Photo Stream on every device signed in to the same iCloud account, including your iPhone.

 When you delete a photo that you shot on your iPhone from My Photo Stream, it is removed from the My Photo Stream collection, but it still remains in the Camera Roll album until you delete it from there.

Shared Photo Streams are new with iOS 6. They let you share photos with selected iCloud users privately, on the Web publicly, or both.

To create a new Shared Photo Stream, do the following:

1. Tap the + button at the upper left of the Photo Stream list. A panel appears, where you can type a name for the new Photo Stream, invite people to share it, and make it available as a public site:

2. Give your new Photo Stream a name. A Shared Photo Stream requires a name.

3. At the top of the screen, tap Create. A new Shared Photo Stream containing no photos and not yet shared with anyone is created and appears in the Photo Stream list.

Once you have a new Shared Photo Stream, you can add photos to it at any time:

1. Tap the Shared Photo Stream in the Photo Stream list. The empty Photo Stream appears, as shown here:

2. Tap Edit, and then tap the Add button that appears at the bottom of the screen. Your Albums list appears.

3. Add photos to your Photo Stream the same way that you add photos to a new album, as described earlier in this chapter. Note that in addition to adding photos from albums, you can add them from your My Photo Stream and from your Events and Faces collections.

4. When you finish adding photos, tap Done. The photos you have tapped appear in the Shared Photo Stream.

Once you have some photos to share, you can share them with other individuals privately, share them on a public web site, or both. (Technically, you can share the Photo Stream at the time you create it, but we think it is impolite, and confusing, to share a Photo Stream with someone else before it contains any photos.)

To share one of your Shared Photo Streams, do the following:

1. In the Photo Stream list, tap the blue arrow at the right of the stream you want to share (refer to Figure 14-4). The Edit Photo Stream screen appears, as shown:

2. Do any of the following:

- Tap Add People, and enter the e-mail addresses of the people you want to invite. Use the blue + button to choose people from your Contacts list. Tap Add when you're done; an invitation e-mail is sent immediately to the people you specified. Invitees must have an iCloud account and an Apple ID to view the Shared Photo Stream to which they have been invited.

- Turn on Public Website and then tap Share Link. A Sharing menu appears, as shown next. You can share the link via e-mail or text message, post the link on Facebook or Twitter, or copy the link to the clipboard and paste it in another app. Anyone can view the Shared Photo Stream in a web browser.

3. At the top of the Edit Photo Stream screen, tap Photo Stream to return to the Photo Stream list when you have finished.

You can use the Edit Photo Stream screen at any time to modify the list of people you have invited to the Shared Photo Stream, to turn the public web site on or off, and to delete the Photo Stream with the Delete Photo Stream button. When you delete a Shared Photo Stream, both the Photo Stream and its contents are removed from the devices of the people with whom you have shared it; however, if any of them has copied any of the photos, those copies remain.

Viewing Events, Faces, and Places

You do not create events, faces, or places collections on your iPhone; instead, these come from your computer when you sync photos from it with your iPhone.

Photo programs on a computer can group and organize photos according to *events*. Often, events photos are grouped on the same day they are taken, but you can create events that span many days if you want and the photo program allows it. Events photos on your iPhone appear in a list like the one shown next, which you can see when you tap Events at the bottom of the Photos app's screen. Tap an Event in the Events list to see thumbnails of the photos in the event; you can view individual photos in an event the same way you view photos in albums.

Faces are collections of photos that all contain a facial image of a specified person; such collections are created on a computer that uses facial recognition software to organize photos (iPhoto on the Mac, for example, can do this). You can sync such collections with your iPhone; when you tap Faces at the bottom of the Photos app screen, you see a list of Faces collections like the one shown here. (Some faces and names have been blurred to protect privacy in this illustration.) As with events and albums, you can tap a name in the Faces list to see thumbnails of the photos, and you can tap a thumbnail to see the photo it represents.

Places organizes photos by where they were taken, based upon information stored with the photos. When you tap Places at the bottom of the Photos app's screen, you see a map similar to the one shown next. A red pin indicates locations that have photos associated with them. You can double-tap the map, or pinch outward, to zoom in closer on the map. When you do, some pins may resolve into several pins as the map's level of details increases.

Tap a pin to see a label appear, displaying the number of photos associated with a location. Tap the label to see the thumbnails for that location, and tap a thumbnail to view an individual picture.

15

Shoot and Edit Videos

We've all seen it on TV and in the movies: crowds of people holding up their cell phones to capture video of celebrities, crime scenes, or just about anything that grabs their attention. With your iPhone's 1080p high-definition iSight (rear-facing) video camera, you have the best (at the time we're writing this) cell phone video camera available. And the FaceTime HD (front-facing) video camera is no slouch at 720p, matching or exceeding the quality of the majority of other phone video cameras.

 Now You Know **Video vs. Screen Resolution**

The FaceTime HD camera supports 720p video, which means that each frame has a resolution of 1280×720 pixels. If you delved through the technical specifications for your iPhone 5, you might remember that the iPhone 5's screen resolution is 1136×640. This means that the FaceTime HD camera captures video that is larger by about 12.5 percent in each dimension than your iPhone screen. The situation is even more pronounced when you look at video taken by the iSight camera on the back, which captures 1080p (1920×1080 pixels) video, about 1.7 times as many pixels as can be displayed on the iPhone's screen in each dimension, or almost three times as many pixels, total.

Keep in mind, however, that even though you have the best of breed, your iPhone's video cameras still aren't really competitive with dedicated high-definition camcorders that have optical zoom and a number of adjustable settings for focus, white balance, and so forth. The front camera is focused for a typical arm's length for video chatting, and the rear camera is intended for more distant objects being the focus. Additionally, only the rear camera has access to the LED flood light functionality (the same LED that functions as a flash for the rear still camera we discussed in Chapter 14).

Using the Video Cameras

Almost all the functionality of the still camera controls discussed in Chapter 14 is replicated in the controls for the video camera, because they're both in the same app. So start by launching the Camera app. First, switch to the video functionality by toggling the still/video switch to the movie camera icon. See Figure 15-1 for the various controls.

- Switch from the front to the rear camera by tapping the on-screen switch cameras button.

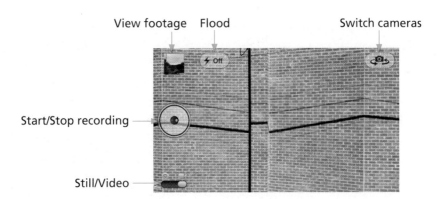

Figure 15-1 *Video camera controls*

- Turn the flood light on (if using the iSight camera) by tapping the on-screen On/Off button with the lightning bolt.

- Start/stop recording by tapping the silver button with the red dot in its center (the red dot blinks while you're recording).

- Watch your recorded video after switching to the Photos app by tapping the thumbnail image at the upper-left corner in landscape orientation or the lower-left of the screen in portrait orientation.

- Change the focal point for the camera by tapping to move the blue square to the desired location.

Again, as with still pictures, the footage you record is placed in your Photos app's Camera Roll.

 If you have the opportunity to do so, you should start recording a second (or more) before the action starts and continue until a second or two after the end of the scene. In this way, you are sure to record everything you want, and you can then trim off any extraneous material, leaving your entire scene intact. At least, that's what our friends in the motion picture industry taught us, and we don't end up missing any parts of our scenes.

Mentioning trimming leads us into the next topic: editing. The Photos app provides (very limited) video editing functionality. You can trim from either end and then either save over the original or save as a new clip. To trim in the Photos app, tap and hold on the preview strip of frames at the top. Yellow handles appear. Drag the yellow handles to the trim point and then tap Trim. At this point, you are offered the options of saving over the original or saving as a new clip. Remember that video is space-consumptive and saving as a new clip, if it is fairly long, can consume a fair chunk of your storage.

Make a Movie in iMovie

Editing video means different things to different people. For many, especially those who got their start with film, editing is the trimming and arrangement of the footage that has been recorded. Those who are videographers of the digital era also include adjusting lighting; adding and removing audio, as well as adjusting its volume; and performing special effects on the video.

To the traditionalist, the core editing functions—trimming, cutting, and splicing your clips—can all be performed in the optional iMovie app. The advantage of using the tools in iMovie is that you can perform these tasks without the risk of slicing your fingers, messing with tape, or having scraps of celluloid scattered across your desk and floor. And as a bonus, you can undo anything you did if you change your mind or make a mistake. Reassembling mistakenly sliced film is much more difficult than assembling any jigsaw puzzle we've seen, but backtracking in iMovie is simplicity itself, thanks to Undo.

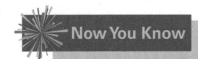 **iMovie Through the Years**

Apple introduced the first version of iMovie with the iMac DV in 1998. (Believe us when we say that 14 or 15 years in the computer industry is a very long time.) Since then, in all its versions, iMovie has remained the standard against which all other consumer video-editing software is compared, with the software being compared to it almost invariably falling short. Apple has released an iOS-based version of iMovie ($4.99 at the time we're writing this), which we would have called "iMovie Lite." It's a very good product for the iOS platform, but it lacks many features of its Mac-based namesake; so if you're familiar with iMovie on OS X, don't expect the iOS version to be a complete solution. In fact, we consider it useful for only the most basic operations on an iPhone's small screen, but much more usable on an iPad.

Because it's easier, and generally faster, to edit video on the much larger screen that a computer offers, we recommend you avail yourselves of that option or use the software on an iPad, when possible. Having larger screen devices, ourselves, and stubby fingers and aging eyes, we use iMovie on our Macs except for really simple chores such as trimming some footage from the beginning or end of a clip.

Start a Project

Tap iMovie on your Home screen and you'll see the marquee screen, where you start a new project or trailer, as shown in Figure 15-2.

Figure 15-2 *Start here to create a new iMovie project.*

Follow the instruction and tap the + icon. You'll see the choices to start a New Project, a New Trailer, or Cancel (which takes you back to the previous screen).

Tap New Project and you arrive at the editing table, shown here both in landscape and portrait orientations. This should provide another impetus to work in landscape as much as possible.

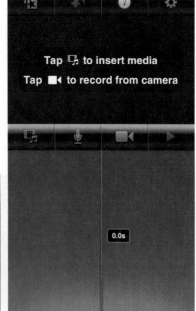

Tap the Settings button to choose an iMovie theme (canned transitions and effects) to your project. iMovie provides eight themes (at the time we're writing this), as shown. iMovie on the Mac offers many more themes, including the option to use no theme at all (which is Dennis's preferred setting), an unavailable option in the iOS version.

If you already have movie clips you want to use in your Photos library, tap the Add Media button. If you want to take new footage at this point, tap the Record from Camera button. Assuming that you want to add media, iMovie will request permission to grab video from your library (but only the first time). Click OK.

Select the clip you want and adjust the selection, if desired, by dragging the ends of the yellow border. To add it to your project, tap the blue, curved down-arrow button superimposed on the selection.

You can also add photos to your project to use, for example, as freeze frames (a la TV series "NCIS") or to create a slideshow. Drag the yellow handles to modify the time the photo remains onscreen. You can also pinch in or outward to adjust how much of the image is used.

 If the photo's aspect ratio differs from that of the movie frame, iMovie pans across the image during playback to show the entire image.

If you want to bring in audio to use as background music, tap the Audio button at the bottom of the screen when adding media. You'll be presented with supplied sound effects as well as the contents of your Music library, as shown:

Tap the appropriate category and pick your sound or music by tapping, and it appears below the video portion of your timeline, as shown here:

Additionally, you can tap Record Audio to narrate a segment.

Tap the Play button whenever you want to preview your movie. You can go back and add to the movie, cut footage from the movie, move clips around, and so forth.

When you have your movie the way you want it, you can return to the My Projects (marquee) screen and publish it to a variety of online sources or add it to your computer's iTunes library (as shown next) by tapping the Share button.

Tap the marquee text that says "My Project" and it highlights, the keyboard appears, and you can type in a more appropriate name for the project.

The High-Low Summary of iPhone Video

As we stated in the beginning of this chapter, the cameras in your iPhone 5 are the best we've seen anywhere on a smartphone. They produce excellent footage and are extremely easy to use. They're not HD video camcorders with all the bells and whistles, but they're omnipresent, not requiring you to tote along a much larger device (probably in a shoulder bag) and fumble to get set up and running when you come across scenes you want to preserve.

We know we've grumbled about video editing on the iPhone. We'd like to stress that this isn't due to any failings of the iMovie software. iMovie is actually, at least in our opinions, the cream of the crop when it comes to video editing software on a mobile device. The fact is that video contains a lot of content, and the iPhone screen, while larger and much sharper than that on most other mobile devices, is still only 4 inches diagonally. The size of the screen constrains what can be accomplished with a touchscreen interface, especially for people with broad fingers (or without perfect vision).

If you have only the iPhone available to do your editing and movie composition, you can, with care and patience, accomplish a great deal and produce quality videos. On the other hand, if you have a Mac with its iMovie software, an iPad with the same iMovie that's on your iPhone (remember, buy it once and use it on all your iOS devices), or even a Windows PC with Premiere Elements (version 11 is our favorite), you can accomplish a lot more, more quickly, and with greater ease.

A

Troubleshooting

Nothing in this world is perfect. Although your iPhone is a finely crafted piece of equipment, it can, like anything else, exhibit flaws. Nor is the software that runs on your iPhone perfect: that, too, can have occasional problems. This appendix provides some tips on what to do when something goes wrong and offers suggestions on how to protect your data so that any flaws and problems you encounter amount to inconveniences instead of disasters.

Back Up Your iPhone

This is the number one safety tip we can offer to anyone who uses an iPhone: back it up. You can always get another iPhone if the one you have is damaged or broken, and you can always replace the software and purchased media on it as well, as you learned in Part IV of this book. What is less easy to replace is the information you create yourself.

Some information on your iPhone is automatically backed up if you have followed our suggestions in this book. For example, if you use iCloud, Gmail, or an IMAP account of any sort for your mail (as described in Chapter 3), the mail on your iPhone is only a copy: your mail remains on the servers of your e-mail service provider so you can get it again (unless, of course, you choose to delete it yourself). Similarly, if you use iCloud, Exchange, CalDAV, and similar methods for creating and accessing contact and calendar information (see Chapter 7), your contacts and calendars are also stored on external servers as well as on your iPhone: should you lose your iPhone or drop it into a puddle of water, you can usually recover all of your contact and calendar information from those sources. And if you regularly sync your iPhone with iTunes, as described in Chapter 9, the information you sync with iTunes can be restored from iTunes.

However, the information that individual apps store for themselves resides only on your iPhone: to get that kind of information back in case of a disaster, you first must have a backup of it. Fortunately, Apple provides two backup methods you can use to back up: an iCloud backup and an iTunes backup. Even better, once you enable one of these methods the backup happens automatically. For iCloud backups, it happens when you plug your iPhone in to be charged; it is locked, and it is connected to the Internet through a Wi-Fi connection. For iTunes backups, it happens when you connect your iPhone to your computer to sync it, either with the USB cable or wirelessly if you set up syncing over Wi-Fi with iTunes.

To enable iCloud backups (assuming you have an iCloud account, of course), do the following:

1. Launch the Settings app and then tap iCloud.

2. On the iCloud screen, flick down to the Storage & Backup setting and tap it.

3. On the Storage & Backup screen, turn on iCloud Backup.

To enable iTunes backups, do the following:

1. Open iTunes on your computer.

2. Connect your iPhone to your computer with the cable that came with your iPhone.

3. Select your iPhone within iTunes and, on the Summary screen in iTunes, click Back Up to this Computer.

Now, should disaster strike, you can restore your iPhone's data either to an erased iPhone or to a new iPhone from your backup.

For more information on how to back up and to restore your iPhone, consult the following Apple Support document: "iOS: How to back up your data and set up as a new device" (http://support.apple.com/kb/HT4137).

Restart to Handle Misbehaving Apps and Other Problems

Sometimes, because of a bug or an unanticipated situation, an app can lock up on you and become unresponsive to taps or other gestures. You may not even be able to close the app: if an app is truly locked, the Home button itself may become unresponsive. Or what if your phone exhibits other problems, such as not being able to find a signal or not showing when you have new voicemail? In those cases, you can force your iPhone to restart, which often solves the problem.

Here's how to force your iPhone to restart:

1. Press and hold down the Sleep/Wake button at the top of your iPhone.

2. At the same time, press and hold the Home button.

3. Wait about ten seconds until the iPhone screen goes black and then shows the white Apple logo.

4. Release both buttons. The iPhone restarts itself, returning to the Home screen after a minute or two.

 Although your iPhone can operate for weeks or even months without needing to be restarted, you can avoid some problems if you restart it every so often. To restart your iPhone without forcing it, press and hold the Sleep/Wake button for a few seconds until the Slide To Power Off slider appears. Slide it to power your iPhone off, and then when you're ready to turn it back on, press the Sleep/Wake button for a few seconds until the Apple logo appears on the screen.

Close Misbehaving Apps with the Multitasking Bar

Sometimes an app can seem to be functional, but it may not respond to taps or gestures properly, even when you quit the app and restart it. Sometimes the problem can be subtle: a sound-playing app might not play sounds, might play sounds no matter what you do, might refuse to start up properly, or it might do something else that just doesn't seem quite right.

Such problems are usually caused by corrupted app state information: When you quit an app on your iPhone, the app stores the state it was in when it quits so it can return to that state when you start it again. For example, when you are reading a book with iBooks and quit the app, iBooks stores its state so the next time you start it you see the book and the page you were reading when you closed the app.

You can force an app to discard its saved state information and start fresh the next time you open it by using the multitasking bar. Here's how:

1. Click the Home button once to return to the Home screen.

2. Double-click the Home button to reveal the multitasking bar. This bar shows the apps you have recently used, with the most recently used app on the left.

3. Press and hold on one of the app icons in your iPhone's multitasking bar until the multitasking bar goes into jiggle mode. A red circle with a white minus sign appears at the upper-left corner of each app icon in the multitasking bar.

4. Tap the red circle to delete the app from the multitasking bar. Note that this action doesn't delete the app from your iPhone; it only removes the app from the multitasking bar.

5. Double-click the Home button. The next time you open the app, it starts fresh.

Some apps can continue to perform certain functions even when you quit them. For example, certain apps may need to maintain a network connection even while you're using another app. Removing the app from the multitasking bar also stops any such background activity performed by that app and can often help you solve otherwise unexplained problems, such as having the battery drain too quickly or excessive mobile network usage.

AppleCare+

When you buy a new iPhone, you get a limited hardware warranty for one year that can cover your iPhone has hardware issues. In addition, a new iPhone comes with 90 days of complimentary technical telephone support from Apple to address software issues or to answer questions.

You can extend the one-year hardware warranty and the 90-day technical telephone support to two years if you purchase Apple's AppleCare+ coverage within 30 days of your iPhone purchase. AppleCare+ not only protects you from manufacturing flaws but even for two incidents of accidental damage (subject to a $49 per-incident fee). AppleCare+ coverage costs $99 in the United States; the amount of coverage and cost may differ for other locations.

Is it worth it? It depends. If you are the sort of person who has "bad luck" with digital devices, the coverage may very well be worth it. In any case, you should investigate the coverage that Apple offers to see if it is right for you. You can find out more about AppleCare+ at http://www.apple.com/support/products/iphone.html.

Index